7.95

Israel

Editor Lesley Firth
Assistant Editor Julia Kirk
Design Robert Wheeler
Picture Research Maggie Colbeck
Production Rosemary Bishop
Illustrations Hayward Art Group
               John Shackell
               Tony Payne
Maps Matthews and Taylor Associates

Photographic sources Key to positions
of illustrations: *(T)* top, *(C)* centre,
(B) bottom, *(L)* left, *(R)* right.
Nick Birch: *23(TL)*. Photoarchives Yael
Braun: *2-3, 6-7, 8(BL), 9(BR), 10(T),
11(TR), 11(BR), 13(TR), 13(BR),
15(T), 15(BL), 15(BR), 16(BL), 16(BR),
17(TR), 17(BR), 18(TL), 18(BR),
19(TR), 20(TL), 20(BL), 21(BL),
21(TR), 21(BR), 22(BL), 22(BR),
23(BR), 23(TR), 24(T), 25(TL),
25(BL), 25(TR), 25(BR), 27(TR),
28(BR), 31(TL), 32(BR), 33(BL), 32(TL),
33(TR), 33(BR), 34(BR), 35(TL),
35(TR), 37(CR), 42(T), 42(B), 43(TL),
43(BR), 44(TL), 45(TL), 45(TR),
45(B), 46(CL), 47(TL), 47(BL), 48(T),
48(BR), 50(TR), 51(TL), 51(TR),
51(BR), 52(TL), 52(TR), 52(BL),
53(BL), 53(BR)*. British Museum:
35(BL). Camera and Pen: *26(BL),
31(TR), 36(T)*. Central Zionist
Archives: *41(TR), 41(CL), 41(BR)*.
Colour Library International: *30(T)*.
Mike Hickin: *53(TL)*. Embassy of Israel:
*9(TR), 9(BL), 11(TL), 26(BR), 35(BR),
43(BL), 44(TR), 49(TL)*. Israel
Government Tourist Office: *8(BR)*:
photo Michael Peto; *49(TR)*. Jewish
Observer: *38(TL), 40(BR), 41(TL)*.
Mansell Collection: *37(BL), 38(BL)*.
Radio Times Hulton Picture Library:
39(T), 39(BR). SEF: *10(B), 37(BR)*.
Ronald Sheridan: *14(T), 30(BR)*.
UNRWA: *49(BR)*. Weizmann Archives:
38(BR). ZEFA: *12(B), 13(BL), 18(TR),
18(BL), 21(TL), 26(TL), 27(BL),
27(BR), 28(TL), 28(BL), 29(TL),
29(TR), 43(TR), 43(CR), 44(BR),
46(TL), 46(BL), 47(TR), 47(CL),
47(BR), 49(BL), 50(B), 51(BL), 53(TR)*.

First published 1977
Macdonald Educational Ltd.
Holywell House, Worship Street,
London E.C.2

© Macdonald Educational Ltd. 1977

ISBN 0-382-06146-2

Published in the United
States by Silver Burdett
Company, Morristown, N.J.
1977 Printing

Library of Congress
Catalog Card No. 77-088352

The endpaper shows a desert scene near
Ein Gedi.

The photograph opposite the list of
contents shows Independence Day
celebrations at the Tower of David,
Jerusalem.

Israel

the land and its people

Danah Zohar

Macdonald Educational

Contents

From the ends of the earth

An ancient dream

"Next year in Jerusalem…" has been prayed hopefully by Jews each Passover during their nearly 2,000 years of exile in foreign lands. The phrase became the password for Jewish survival despite the persecutions they endured during centuries of dispersion throughout the world. They never gave up the dream that one day they would return to Israel. There has always been a fairly large Jewish community in the land of Israel, no matter who governed the country.

Early pioneers

The first of modern Israel's new immigrants began arriving in the late nineteenth century. Most came from Russia or Eastern Europe. They came in small numbers, and were driven by their imagination to rebuild the Promised Land.

The first task of the new pioneers, known as Zionists, was simply survival. In the harsh conditions which greeted them, that was not so simple. Their second task was to prepare the way for hundreds of thousands of other Jews to follow. This required the draining of swamps, building of hospitals and schools, ridding the land of malaria, and laying the first foundations of a political and economic structure for the future state. But until the horrors of this century, the number of immigrants was relatively small.

Ingathering of the exiles

With the mass slaughter of Jews wherever Hitler's armies struck, many looked to the new Israel as their only hope of survival. The shattered remnants of European Jewry began pouring into Palestine by every available means. As the War ended, European Jews were joined by several hundred thousand Jews from Arab lands such as Morocco, Tunisia, Egypt and Iraq.

The "ingathering of the exiles" became the central task of the new State of Israel, which won its independence in 1948. Jews from nearly every country on earth, speaking many languages, knew they would find a home, welcome and help in the new Jewish state.

The Law of Return decreed that every Jew could automatically become a citizen of his land upon arrival. For many, it was the first time they had ever enjoyed citizenship anywhere.

Nation of immigrants

Israel today is still a nation of immigrants, a vast melting pot of the cultures from which her citizens have come. But the new, native generation is catching up quickly.

Where the immigrants came from (1948–1972)			
Eastern Europe		**Africa**	
Bulgaria	48,660	Algeria	13,135
Russia	65,882	South Africa	8,097
Yugoslavia	8,092	Tunisia	46,885
Poland	156,195	Libya	34,347
Others	279,029	Morocco	255,633
		Egypt	37,922
Western Europe		Others	1,543
Italy	4,131		
United Kingdom	16,417	**America**	
Belgium	3,915	United States	47,167
Germany	11,922	Canada	5,281
Holland	4,051	Argentina	24,669
France	31,932	Brazil	6,635
Switzerland	2,192	Mexico	1,586
Spain	660	Chile	3,805
Others	10,709	Uruguay	3,709
		Unregistered	5,531
Asia			
India	21,645	**Oceania**	3,186
Iran	63,077		
Turkey	56,463	**Unregistered**	22,342
Others	190,483		

► A Yemenite family gather round their kettle. The Yemenites returned to Israel via a massive airlift called Operation Magic Carpet

▼ Jews have come to Israel from countries all over the world, including India.

Origins of the Jewish population in 1973

Though Israel is still a nation of immigrants, its native *sabra* population is growing fast.

Born in Europe and the Americas

27·2%

Born in Israel (Sabras)

47·9%

Born in Asia and Africa (mainly Arab countries)

24·9%

► These university students from different backgrounds will help to lead their new nation.

▼ A Moroccan immigrant proudly wears the costume of her native Atlas mountains.

► An Israeli Bedouin family. The Bedouin are an Arab people who have followed a nomadic life for many centuries.

Land of contrasts

Ancient and modern

Israel is a striking patchwork of differences. Though it is one of the world's smallest countries, it contains within its borders some of the greatest variety found anywhere on earth.

Perhaps the most immediately noticeable contrast is that between the ancient and modern. Scenes unchanged from Biblical times often exist side by side with the fullest expression of twentieth century life.

In just the short journey from modern Ben Gurion Airport into equally modern Tel Aviv, one passes through thousands of years of history. Many visitors to Israel have suffered near heart-failure as their taxis have passed all too close to some wandering camel or an Arab peasant astride his donkey. These symbols of the past seem to take no notice of the busy modern world around them.

A varied climate

Israel's climate and landscape are immensely varied within very short distances. Bordered on the south by the Red Sea and the Negev Desert, the country has the Mediterranean Sea and a rich coastal plain on its west.

Going inland, one comes to the rugged foothills of the Judaean Hills and Desert amongst which Jerusalem is nestled. North, beyond the arid stretches of Samaria, the land suddenly turns soft and green. This is the one-time swampland of Galilee, now a flourishing agricultural area.

On the country's far eastern border, there is the eerie bleakness of the Dead Sea region, the lowest point on the earth's surface.

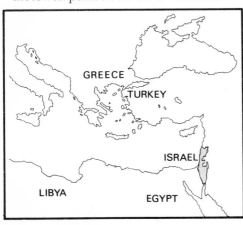

▲ These Spring marchers enjoy the rich and varied landscape of the green hills leading up to Jerusalem from Tel Aviv's coastal plain. There are more than 2,000 species of plant life in Israel, several dozens of which are found in this one small area.

▼ Tel Aviv was founded on a Mediterranean sand dune in 1909 by a group of Jewish pioneers. It quickly grew to become Israel's largest and most modern city. It is the nation's commercial, industrial and communications centre.

◀ Holiday-makers on their way home from the popular ski slopes of snow-capped Mount Hermon pass by Arab residents of the Golan Heights. Syria lies just beyond.

▼ An Arab shepherd grazes his sheep on the sparse shrubbery of the Judaean Desert. The soft, rose-brown hills of Judaea rise up behind him. The winding road leads to Jerusalem, whose minarets and spires can be seen crowning the hill tops.

▲ Eerie salt pillars stand like a watchful army over the strange, uninhabitable terrain of the Dead Sea, the lowest point on earth. Perhaps one is Lot's wife, who was turned into a pillar of salt according to the Biblical story. Salt mining is a major Israeli industry.

Haifa

Lake Kinneret

Tel Aviv

JORDAN

Jerusalem

Dead Sea

NEGEV

Area under Israeli administration

MT. HERMON (TO THE SNOW SLOPES)

The Israeli character

A nation of individualists

Israel is a nation of eccentrics and individualists, so in some senses the national character is as varied as the number of "characters" who make up the population. Add to this the rich backdrop of ethnic variety and a large number of minority groups, and Israel can be seen as a very complex nation indeed. Still, some traits stand out as general enough to be noticed.

The generation gap

Israelis, young and old, display a great deal of personal and national self-confidence, and parents and children alike are proud of the young nation they have built. But despite the shared effort, Israel's generation gap between the parents who came from other lands and their children, who have known no other home but Israel, is increasingly noticeable. The immigrant generation cannot help having memories of life in other lands. They sometimes look back, and this affects their ideas and values in the new country. The generation born in Israel, which is now providing the leadership, is more a part of the Middle East.

▼ Young soldiers line up to catch a "tramp" home or back to base. Hitch hiking is very common in Israel, and giving soldiers lifts is just part of good citizenship.

A bit prickly

Native-born Israelis are known as *sabras* named after a local fruit that is soft on the inside but hard and prickly on the outside. It is a good description of the bustling and abrasive outward personality of young Israelis. To outsiders, they often seem brash or "cocky" but once one has the opportunity to get beneath this surface appearance, it is easy to see that most *sabras* are quite sensitive people, always preoccupied with self-appraisal and eager to learn from, and about, other people.

Gregarious

Israelis love doing things in crowds. Every street corner offers the opportunity for impromptu theatre as groups of people gather to gesticulate wildly while discussing anything from the price of bread to great national issues.

Talking is probably Israel's greatest national sport. Whether gathering in one of the many cafes, or at home, Israelis seldom miss any opportunity to gossip or argue. Politics is a particularly favourite subject for these fireside orators, and nearly every Israeli thinks that he could be running the country better than the Prime Minister.

Irreverent

Perhaps it is because every Israeli believes he should be running the country that there is such lack of deference to authority. Israelis are proud of their laws and political institutions, but a sense that every citizen is just as equal as any other pervades the national character.

▲ Exuberant film-goers often show their enthusiasm by rolling bottles down the aisles!

▲ The older generation often benefits from the self-confidence of the *sabras*.

▲ Israelis read more books and newspapers than perhaps any other nation.

▼ Groups gather at pavement cafes to indulge in a favourite pastime, political argument.

▼ Israelis, young and old, have a strong sense of duty and civic pride. There is no problem recruiting volunteers for any community need. Here, a schoolgirl does her part guarding a pedestrian crossing.

▲ Youth takes to the streets for a colourful students' day parade down Jerusalem's Jaffa Road. Over half of Israel's population is under 25, giving the national character a strong youthful accent.

▼ Age and tradition also have their place. The sharp contrast of old and new ways can be seen in every town and street. Here, Arab men in traditional and western headgear sit side by side to smoke waterpipes.

A nation shaped by religion

Israel's religious tradition

As the land of the Bible and the Koran, holy to three of the world's great religions, Israel is a nation where religion plays a strong role. Every part of Israel has at some time been walked over or fought upon by holy men, prophets and religious warriors. The atmosphere of the country is alive with a special feeling bred by thousands of years of religious passion and struggle.

For a new visitor to Israel, the first impression of seeing road signs that point to such places as Bethlehem, Jerusalem, Beersheba and Sodom can be a strange one. The sense of reality is not increased by the sight of monks whizzing by on motor scooters, their robes flapping in the breeze, or of Arab waiters suddenly disappearing from serving tables to prostrate themselves towards Mecca in prayer.

In Jerusalem itself, the city most dominated by religion, there is always some religious sound carried on the breeze: the cry of the muezzin echoing verses of the Koran from minarets, the rhythmic chanting of Jewish prayers rising from synagogues and the Western Wall, and the constant peal of church bells.

Religion in the modern state

Judaism is the dominant faith in Israel, and it has shaped even the political structure of the modern state. Jewish nationhood itself is a religious concept based on the belief that God sought a people who would accept and live by His Law in this world. It was when the Jews accepted the Law that they ceased being scattered desert tribes and became a nation.

Religious political parties sit in Israel's parliament and claim some 10-12 per cent of the national vote. Questions such as "Who is a Jew?" and Sabbath observance are often burning national issues, and have on occasion led to street riots.

Fifteen per cent of Israel's population is non-Jewish and includes Christians, Muslims, Druses, Karaites and Samaritans. Each faith practises its beliefs with complete freedom, and all customs to do with birth, marriage and death are left in the hands of the respective religious community leaders.

▲ Jews gather to pray at Jerusalem's Western Wall, the most sacred site of their faith.

▼ The Torah (Five Books of Moses) is the source of laws governing Orthodox Jewish life.

Religious affiliations, 1973

Muslims 11·2%
Christians 2·4%
Druses and others 1·3%
Jews 85·1%

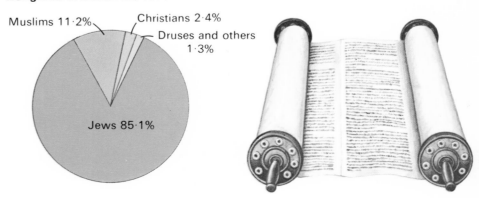

▲ Christian pilgrims walk along the Via Dolorosa (Way of Sorrow) in Jerusalem each Friday morning. They follow the path taken by Christ as He bore His cross to Calvary. There are some 75,000 Christians living in Israel, the vast majority being Arabs who are Catholic or Greek Orthodox.

◄ A Muslim Arab sits reading the Holy Koran inside a mosque in northern Akko. There are more than 328,000 Muslims in Israel. The Muslim holy day is Friday, but each day, 5 times a day, the community is called to prayer by a verse of the Koran being cried out from the several hundred minarets throughout the land.

► A Druse *khadi* (judge) reflects on a decision. The Druses are a mysterious sect that broke away from Islam 1,000 years ago. They have kept their religion separate and secret ever since. Druses never marry out-siders, but their close knit communities remain loyal to the needs of whatever society offers them shelter.

Customs and superstitions

A rich store of custom

Custom and superstition have played a central role in Jewish life throughout the ages. The Bible is as rich in folklore as it is deep in religious inspiration, and nothing has happened since to change this. As the centuries pass, the treasure of custom and folklore grows, and even the most modern and secular of Israeli Jews practise some of the old ways.

Because Jews have lived scattered around the world for two thousand years, their customs have naturally absorbed many of the traditions and superstitions of the peoples among whom they lived. Thus Israeli custom is a colourful patchwork of the folkways of many lands, though in each case the "borrowed" custom has been given a distinctly Jewish flavour.

▶ Passover, or the Season of Freedom, is one of the most important festivals of the Jewish year. It celebrates the freedom of the ancient Hebrews from Egyptian bondage. For modern Israelis the celebration has an added meaning. Here, a Persian family celebrates the traditional *Seder,* or Passover meal.

▼ Hiking is one of Israel's great national passions. Each Spring, people of all ages join a 3-day march through the hills of Judaea and Samaria. Those who finish the march parade triumphantly through Jerusalem.

The Western Wall

One of the first widely-held beliefs a visitor might notice in modern Israel is the custom of tucking a note expressing some heart-felt wish into a crack in Jerusalem's Western Wall, the only surviving remnant of the destroyed Second Temple. Devout Jews believe these messages are prayers to God. A famous photograph of General Moshe Dayan, taken just after the Israeli Army had recaptured the Old City and the Western Wall during the 1967 Six Day War, shows the General tucking such a note into a crevice in the wall.

Another common custom is that if a Jew is saved miraculously from death, he must instantly give to charity. Most of the more important customs and superstitions of Israeli life are related to the crucial events of birth, coming of age, marriage and death. The ceremonies associated with each are a rich blend of age-old superstition and firmly established ritual custom.

Circumcision and marriage

Circumcision, the most sacred and ancient rite of Judaism, is attended by such folk customs as keeping the ritual knife under the mother's pillow the night before, or keeping an all-night watch against the evil spirits. But the heart of the ritual is that it must take place on the eighth day after the boy's birth, during the hours of daylight, and in the presence of ten adult Jewish men.

Marriage is also steeped in many strange and old customs. The bridal couple are joined under the *Huppah,* or canopy, a survival of the ancient bridal bower in which newlyweds used to be secluded after the ceremony.

Another ancient marriage custom—that the community as a whole should join in wedding celebrations—has been gladly carried on in modern Israel. Any wedding party is likely to be graced with several uninvited guests who have just dropped in for the food, drink and dancing.

▲ When a Jewish boy reaches 13, he becomes *Bar Mitzvah*—"a man of duty" The ceremony is the most important in his life until he marries, and marks him as a man with full responsibilities in the life of the synagogue.

► Orthodox Jews build a fire and dance round the grave of Rabbi Simeon ben Yochai on Lag B'omer to remember the day he revealed the secrets of Jewish mysticism to his disciples. Though practised as a Jewish festival the fire observance is actually an ancient heathen ceremony.

► Weddings are the most festive occasions in Israeli life. Each national group has its own special customs and dress, as with the Yemenite couple here, but song and dance are features of every marriage.

▼ A familiar sight on any street corner, the beggar stands ready to accept alms. Israeli beggars are not humble, and often read from scripture to remind passers-by that it is a divine duty to give to the poor.

Family life

▲ A Bedouin Arab family gathers in its tent for the evening meal. For Arabs, the close knit family is the basic social unit.

▲ Kibbutz children visit their parents' rooms for a few hours at the end of the working day. The children sleep in their own quarters.

▼ A *sabra* (native Israeli) family enjoys a picnic lunch in Jerusalem's Independence Park. Saturday is family day for most Israelis.

▼ An Orthodox family goes for a Sabbath walk through Jerusalem's walled lanes. For them, it is a day of quiet togetherness.

Close-knit families

The family has always been the basic unit of Jewish life, and this tradition has carried on in modern Israel. Though family lifestyles and attitudes vary among the various immigrant groups which make up Israel's population, the close-knit family group is a prominent feature of Israeli society as a whole.

Eastern Jewish families are usually large, often having eight or ten children. Families with a western background tend to be much smaller. Secular families observe the major Jewish festivals as holidays, but religious families organize their daily and weekly routine around the rituals laid down in Jewish Law. Kibbutz families lead a very different life. The parents live in their own bungalows and the children are brought up separately in the Children's House.

Whatever their differences, for most Israeli families the evening dinner table is the focal point of family life. Except on the Sabbath, the evening meal is often the only time when the whole family can be together. It is usually a noisy affair, with everyone talking at once about his day, his opinion of the latest political event, or religious issues.

For Jews, Friday evenings and Saturdays (the Sabbath) are usually set aside for visiting relatives, or offering them hospitality.

Tradition and equality

It is traditional among many Israeli families, both Arab and Jewish, for successive generations to live under one roof. Often, a large building is divided into flats, each occupied by some branch of the family. When the new immigrants arrived from Georgian Russia, this tradition became a problem for immigration officials. Among the Georgians, even remote cousins are considered part of the family and they all insisted on being housed together!

Sexual equality is a characteristic of Israeli life perhaps more noticeable than in many other countries. Women can be anything from airforce pilots to prime ministers, but within the home their traditional role remains largely unchanged.

▲ This western immigrant family keeps the modern surroundings and traditions of the country from which it came.

An urban family timetable

BREAKFAST 6.00-7.00 a.m.

SCHOOL-Primary 8.00 a.m.-1.00 p.m.

Secondary 8.00 a.m.-3.00 p.m. Six days a week

WORK Factory 7.00 a.m.-4.00 p.m. Light lunch 1.00 p.m.

Office 8.30 a.m.-4.00 p.m. Light lunch 1.00 p.m.

Shops 9.00-1.00 and 4.00-7.00 Hatzacha (siesta) between

Housewife: shopping and housework 8.00 a.m.-3.00 p.m.

DINNER 8.00 p.m.

Leisure, T.V., homework 8.00-10.30 p.m.

BEDTIME 11.00-12.00 p.m.

Education

▼ A Bedouin youngster rides to school on his donkey. For the Bedouin, formal education is still new, as most families prefer to continue their nomadic life.

Emphasis on youth

Israel is a dynamic young country not yet thirty years old, and youth is emphasised at every level of society. Even Israel's older citizens often look and feel much younger than their equals elsewhere. The energy and enthusiasm required to build a new country so quickly have spread like a pleasant contagious disease, adding a spring to nearly every Israeli's step.

Education a high priority

"Our children are our most important natural resource", former prime minister Golda Meir was fond of saying. Her words are echoed in Israel's budget allocations, for educational expenditure comes second only to defence.

New developments in education

Imagination and skill have gone into devising an educational system which has to deal with enormous differences in the standards of knowledge of immigrant children. Israel's work in education has been especially helpful to Third World countries, and to modern western nations, such as Britain and the United States, which have minority groups of their own that need special facilities for becoming integrated into the larger society.

Education for integration

Because Israel's citizens come from so many countries, creeds and cultures, the first task of education is to weld them into one people. The Hebrew language is one of the most important vehicles for this. Most of Israel's new immigrants arrive with no knowledge of Hebrew. Thus the *ulpan*, or language school, was devised to teach all new arrivals the language of their new country.

Nearly a third of Israel's population is of school age, and school attendance is both free and compulsory from the age of five until 15. Nearly every imaginable need is met: Arabs attend Arab schools, religious Jews attend a range of religious schools, and secular Jews attend state schools.

Beyond the normal primary and secondary school facilities, Israel also offers such alternatives as vocational training schools, agricultural and teacher training colleges, *yeshivot* (religious academies), and child care education programmes. Whatever the need, some educational facility meets it.

Israel also has seven universities, with a total student body of more than 50,000. Arabs may attend these, but plans are now afoot to build another university that will be primarily Arab. The hope is that Arabs from other countries will study there.

▼ Immigrants from different backgrounds, some with no previous education, join small home study groups to learn the basics of the Hebrew language. Such groups also aid social integration.

The Israeli system of education

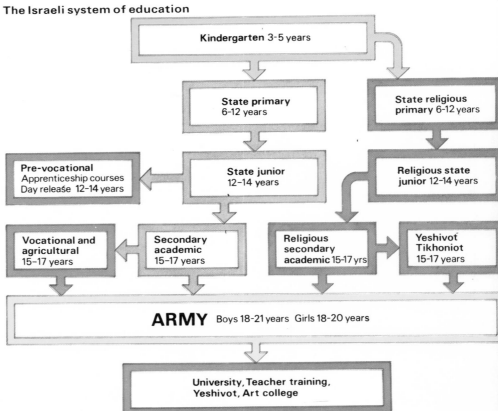

Kindergarten 3-5 years

State primary 6-12 years — State religious primary 6-12 years

State junior 12-14 years — Religious state junior 12-14 years

Pre-vocational Apprenticeship courses Day release 12-14 years

Vocational and agricultural 15-17 years — Secondary academic 15-17 years — Religious secondary academic 15-17 yrs — Yeshivot Tikhoniot 15-17 years

ARMY Boys 18-21 years Girls 18-20 years

University, Teacher training, Yeshivot, Art college

▲ These very young children are attending one of Israel's 4,000 kindergarten classes. One-third of the pre-school population attends kindergarten between the ages of 3 and 5. For 5-year olds it is compulsory. Both fellowship and basic skills are taught.

► Young Orthodox boys are given a lesson in *cheder* (religious school) about the meaning of the festival of Sukkot. Religious children can attend state supported religious schools, which are based on the study of Jewish law and tradition. When older, some will attend *yeshiva*.

► Hebrew University geology students take a field trip in the foothills of the Judaean desert. Geology, and even more so archaeology, are highly popular Israeli interests.

▼ Modern state secondary pupils attend a chemistry lesson in their school laboratory. Science teaching is taken very seriously as Israel needs many research workers.

Media and communication

A news-conscious nation

Several times each day, and late into the evening, Israelis drop their voices and turn towards the radio. It's news time. The radio is turned up and everybody listens. News broadcasts have to be taken seriously in a nation where so much can happen from one hour to the next.

Israelis also read more newspapers per head of population than any other nation, not just Hebrew papers (of which there are eleven dailies), but others in Arabic, English, Russian, German, and many other languages. If a news item differs from one newspaper to the next, Israelis love to argue about which report is the most accurate. Such discussions make cafes very lively places.

The Hebrew language

The most important step towards creating any kind of communications system in Israel was the adoption of one language that could be learned by everyone and used as the nation's official tongue. For religious and historical reasons, the country's Zionist founders settled on Hebrew. The only problem was that Hebrew hadn't been used for daily speech since the exile in 70 A.D. It would have to be updated. This task was largely accomplished by Eliezer Ben-Yehuda, a Russian Jew who emigrated to Palestine in the early years of settlement. He is known as the father of modern Hebrew. Ben-Yehuda compiled a dictionary of the modern language, inventing much as he went along. Where Ben-Yehuda stopped, nearly everyone else began to improvise. So today, it is unusual to find two Israelis who speak Hebrew in exactly the same way.

A multi-lingual nation

Because Israel's citizens come from so many different cultures, the media must accommodate their language needs. News broadcasts on the radio go out in Hebrew, simple Hebrew, Yiddish, English, German, Ladino, Russian and Arabic. Television, which Israel first broadcast in 1968, also has programmes in various languages.

While Hebrew remains the official language of the country, all road signs are printed in Hebrew, Arabic and English, and school children are encouraged to become fluent in all three, no matter which kind of school they attend. The older generation are encouraged to learn as much Hebrew as they can.

The Hebrew Alphabet

LETTER	SOUND	NUMBER
א	–	1
ב	B or V	2
ג	G	3
ד	D	4
ה	H	5
ו	V	6
ז	Z	7
ח	Kh	8
ט	T	9
י	I or Y	10
כ	Kh	20
ל	L	30
מ	M	40
נ	N	50
ס	S	60
ע	–	70
פ	P or F	80
צ	Ts	90
ק	K	100
ר	R	200
ש	Sh or S	300
ת	T or Th	400

◄ Practising his art in much the same way as his predecessors have for centuries, this Torah scribe patiently copies out the Holy Book by hand. Each synagogue keeps several such hand-written scrolls in its Ark.

▼ The largest task of communication in Israel is learning the nation's new language. Here, adult immigrants attend a residential *ulpan* for an intensive course.

▲ This newspaper printed in Hebrew represents the triumph of Zionism's linguistic dream. Creation of a modern Hebrew language, which offers a common tongue for discussing daily events, has given birth to many popular Hebrew journals.

► The spread of modern Hebrew has not prevented Israeli reading matter from being a printed Tower of Babel! This news-stand outside Jerusalem's Damascus Gate shows the international and multi-lingual range of journals available.

◄ Beautifully designed (and multi-lingual) stamps are the pride of Israel's postal service. Designs are changed constantly.

▼ All Israeli street and place signs are written in the nation's 3 "official" languages: Hebrew, Arabic and English. Jaffa Gate, which was sealed for 20 years during Jerusalem's divided Arab/Israeli rule, now symbolizes re-unification.

Celebrations and festivals

Celebrating Independence

All Jewish festivals are fixed according to the lunar system, so that they fall on different dates each year according to our calendar.

The newest festival is Independence Day. It includes a military parade through the streets of Jerusalem. It is opened by a ceremony on Mount Zion in Jerusalem, which also marks the end of the day of remembrance for those who fell in battle.

Passover and Pentecost

Passover (Pessach) commemorates the Exodus from Egypt. The first and last days of Passover are holidays and the five intermediate days are semi-festive. The first evening begins with a service in the home when the youngest child asks four questions so that the father can retell the story of how God brought the children of Israel, led by Moses, from bondage in Egypt to nationhood in the Promised Land.

Pentecost (Shavuot) celebrates the giving of the Ten Commandments on Mount Sinai, and the harvest. Tabernacles (Sukkot), in the autumn, is marked by the setting up of temporary booths in which all meals are eaten for eight days. It concludes with the Rejoicing of the Law, marking the completion of the reading of the Five Books of Moses section-by-section each Sabbath throughout the year.

The Day of Atonement

The Jewish New Year and the Day of Atonement are separated by ten days of penitence. Everyone is called upon to undertake a soul-searching and make their peace for any wrong-doing with both God and their fellow men. The climax is the Day of Atonement, a 24-hour fast, most of which is spent in prayer in the synagogues. There are a few minor festivals. Chanukka commemorates the victory of the Jews against the Greeks. Candles are lit daily for eight days.

Muslim and Christian festivals

The Muslims observe Ramadan around Easter time with special prayers and customs. Christmas and Easter bring many Christians to Nazareth and Bethlehem, and services are held in churches, convents and monasteries.

▲ Celebrating Bikurim (gathering of the first fruits), during the festival of Shavuot, one of Israel's many folk dance groups entertains at a kibbutz.

▼ The events of the Jewish calendar closely follow the year's changes. Many Israeli festivals and holy days have some direct seasonal meaning.

A calendar of Israeli festivals

SPRING

Pessach
Feast of Freedom celebrating the Exodus from Egypt

Purim
Carnivals and street parades

Independence Day
Dancing and singing in the streets
Parades and pageants

SUMMER

Shavuot
Festival of the First Fruits and Giving of the Law on Mount Sinai

WINTER

Tu B'Shvat
New Year of the Trees. Tree planting ceremonies held all over Israel

Chanukka
Feast of Lights commemorating the victory of the Maccabees

AUTUMN

Rosh Hashanah
Jewish New Year

Yom Kippur
Day of Atonement

Sukkot
Feast of Tabernacles and Autumn harvest festival

Simchat Torah
Day of the Rejoicing of the Law Singing and dancing in the synagogues

▲ The candlelight and songs of Chanukka bring joy and festivity to Israel's winter rainy season. These children gather round the traditional menorah on the 8th night.

▶ For Israeli children, the annual Purim parade in Tel Aviv is a grand occasion for wearing costumes and making noise. Purim is a happy freedom celebration marking the defeat of the wicked Haman.

▶ Song and dance are always popular among Israelis, and any occasion is welcomed if it can be danced to. Here, Druse men do a traditional dance to flute music while celebrating one of their holidays.

▼ Sukkot, or the Festival of Booths, is an autumn harvest festival especially popular with children. These youngsters carry miniature sukkot on sticks.

25

East meets West in the market place

▲ Arabs in Jerusalem's Old City stop at one of the many bread stalls to buy rolls of a western type.

From haggling to credit

Israel is not only a geographical crossroads but its population is so mixed that it brings together people of widely various outlooks. When Israel was a part of the Ottoman Empire, before the First World War, it was almost wholly eastern in character. In its narrow, cobbled streets, which still exist in the Old City of Jerusalem and in Safed, the shops were small and goods were often displayed in the streets. Prices were not fixed so customers simply argued with the shopkeeper, sometimes good-humouredly, sometimes heatedly, until they agreed an amount, each thinking they had outdone the other.

In the early part of this century, when most immigrants were Jews from Eastern Europe, their influence began to be felt. The shops began to look like those of Poland, Rumania and Russia. There was less haggling because people were generally poor and lived on credit given by the shops.

Shopping in modern Israel

Since the State of Israel came into being in 1948, immigrants from Western Europe and the United States of America have brought their ideas with them. Moreover, Israelis are a much-travelled people and have learnt from their visits to western countries. So today there is a conglomeration of styles. There is the old-time type of market, notably Carmel in Tel Aviv, and Mahne Yehuda in Jerusalem. Many smaller markets are found elsewhere, especially in the Arab populated towns.

There are American-style supermarkets wherein every conceivable household commodity, as well as all foodstuffs, are sold. In them, prices are fixed and there can be no bargaining. Small shops giving personal service are being put out of business by the supermarkets in Israel.

Roadside stalls and kiosks

Along some of the main roads you will often find stalls with fruit from nearby orchards, where car drivers stop and purchase luscious apples, oranges, plums, grapes and peaches. The prices are usually lower than those charged in shops since there are no overhead expenses to cover.

Another common sight on the roadsides in the towns are kiosks selling drinks, sweets and especially chewing gum—a habit which has caught on among children. Often these kiosks also sell newspapers, which are avidly read. In earlier years, when there were fewer radio sets about, and no television, people often crowded around the kiosks to hear the news.

▲ A familiar sight in any Arab section, this Bethlehem juice vendor sells fruit juice from his shoulder jug.

◀ Watermelon is a summer favourite with all Israelis. These two Nazareth citizens want to choose a good one.

▲ What fun is shopping if you can't do a bit of bargaining? In Israel's old outdoor markets, whether Arab or Jewish, both the shopper and the stall keeper would feel cheated if they didn't haggle first.

▶ The *shuk*, or covered market, in Jerusalem's Old City is a colourful meeting place of East and West. People wearing mini skirts and shorts mix with robed men and women as all look for a bargain.

▲ A fruit and vegetable stall in Jerusalem's Mahane Yehuda (Jewish Market). A keen rival with the Old City's covered market, Mahane Yehuda is always crowded with shoppers looking for the best prices.

▶ In sharp contrast with the traditional outdoor markets and small shops, large western supermarkets are now found in Israel's larger towns. Only the Hebrew lettering betrays this is an Israeli store.

Eating the Israeli way

▲ A kosher butcher prepares cuts of meat according to the strict rules laid down in the Pentateuch. Kosher laws forbid the eating of pork, bacon or shellfish. Meats which may be eaten must be slaughtered as prescribed. Not all Israelis abide by kosher laws, but most public restaurants do.

Dietary laws

The Jews have strict dietary laws which allow them to eat the meat only of animals which chew the cud, which are slaughtered in a special way, and fish which have fins and scales. No milk products can be consumed for some hours after eating meat. Utensils used for preparing meat and milk foodstuffs are kept separate from each other.

It is illegal for Jews to breed pigs or sell pork and bacon but non-Jews are allowed to do so. Muslims also have special laws about eating and slaughtering animals, but they differ from those of Jews.

During the eight days of the Feast of Passover, Jews are forbidden to eat leavened bread, which includes cereals and other by-products. Special arrangements are made for non-Jews to obtain these commodities. Because many Jews no longer observe the dietary laws, they take advantage of this "loophole".

Jewish families who have sojourned in different countries for generations, have often acquired the eating habits of the people among whom they lived, and so the different kinds of food to be found in Israel represent the peoples of the world rather than Jews as such. The result is a variety of choice.

Arabic and kosher dishes

The special foods which have become associated with Israel are Arabic rather than Jewish. Felafel is a general favourite. It is made in small balls and is sold very often at kiosks, where one can see the felafel frying in a bowl. It is put in *pita*, the flat, Arab bread, and this "sandwich" is eaten as you walk along. Eating in the street is considered perfectly in order. Corn on the cob, and watermelon, are other favourites bought and eaten in the street. There are also many oriental restaurants where humous, tehina and kebab are the popular dishes.

There are, however, kosher Jewish restaurants everywhere which serve gefilte (stuffed) fish made of carp, chicken, liver, stuffed neck of chicken and other Eastern European Jewish delicacies. In addition, there are restaurants and hotels where the service and food are similar to the best of western establishments.

Israeli mealtimes

Breakfast can be a meal of sardines, tomatoes, grated carrots, cheese, eggs and toast. The main meal is usually eaten at midday and is followed by a rest. In the evening a light snack is eaten. But in the larger towns, western habits are slowly penetrating and visitors from Britain and the United States can find a "home from home" as easily as those from the east. The Israelis now produce a variety of their own wines, beers and liqueurs.

▼ A Bedouin mother makes bread for her family outside their desert tent. Bread, olives and strong coffee will serve as lunch.

▼ The standard Israeli fare of hard-boiled eggs, pickles and tomatoes is laid out at this picnic for Purim.

▲ This sweets stall, with its rich array of cakes, biscuits and candies, is a familiar sight in any Arab neighbourhood. Arab sweets are very rich.

▲ Israel wouldn't be Israel without its felafel stalls on every street corner. A clear first as the national dish, felafel is usually eaten while walking along.

Cooking the Israeli way

CHOLENT
2 cups dried broad beans
3 lbs beef brisket (for variety, some sausages or other meats can be mixed in)
4 diced onions
3 tablespoons cooking oil or fat
2 teaspoons salt
dash of pepper
dash of ginger
5 cloves
2 teaspoons paprika
1 cup pearl barley
2 tablespoons flour
1 cup red wine
1 cup beef stock

FELAFEL
1 packet felafel mix (available at any Greek food shop)
3 pieces pita bread
houmous or salad dressing
2 tomatoes, finely chopped
1 cucumber, finely chopped
6 pickled chillies, finely chopped
1 onion, finely chopped
dash of salt, pepper, parsley and thyme
2 tablespoons olive oil
1 tablespoon lemon juice

Method for cholent
Soak the beans overnight and then drain before using. Brown the meat and onions in a large casserole with the oil or fat. Add the beans, barley and spices, sprinkle the flour on top, and cover with the wine, beef stock and enough boiling water to fill the casserole at least an inch above the mixture. Cover the casserole tightly and place in a preheated 250°F (Mark 1) oven for 24 hours. The long, slow baking overnight is the secret of a good cholent. From time to time extra water might be added to keep the casserole moist. Serve as the main course, dressed with pickled cucumbers, pickled chillies, and anything else you might choose as a light side dish to complement the rich, heavy flavour of the cholent.

Method for felafel
Mix the felafel (a fine powder of ground chickpeas) with water and allow to stand in a bowl as directed on the packet. While the felafel mix is settling, combine the salad ingredients in a bowl, add the oil, lemon juice and spices, and set to one side. Warm the pita (wrapped in foil) in the oven or grill. In the meantime, form the felafel paste into small balls and deep fry in hot vegetable oil until they are crisp and golden (about 5 minutes). Remove the felafel balls to a draining paper. Cut each piece of warm pita in half. Slice carefully inside each half with a sharp knife to form a pocket. Coat the inside of each pocket with houmous or salad dressing. Place 3 or 4 felafel balls inside, and top with a generous portion of the salad mix.

Jerusalem, the golden city

Sacred city

Jerusalem is a holy city to Jews, Muslims and Christians. It is also the political capital of the modern State of Israel, and home to the Jews and Arabs who live there.

History everywhere

Finding places of historical and religious interest in Jerusalem is no problem. Each step retraces that of some event which shaped the spiritual body of Judaism, Islam or Christianity.

Standing in the beautiful Garden of Gethsemane on the Mount of Olives, where Christ went with his disciples to pray before the Crucifixion, one can look across the Valley of Jehosaphat to the walled Old City and its Golden Gate.

Central to the Old City, which is divided into Jewish, Christian, Muslim and Armenian quarters, is the Temple Mount. On top of the Temple Mount is the golden-domed Mosque of Omar. Inside the Mosque, near the spot which Jews regard as the Holy of Holies, stands a rock in which the hoofprint of a horse is embedded. Muslims believe it was from this rock that the prophet Mohammed rose to heaven.

The base of the Temple Mount is the Western Wall (or Wailing Wall), the last vestige of Judaism's Second Temple, and the most sacred site of Judaism in the world.

Only a short walk from the Western Wall brings Christian pilgrims to the Via Dolorosa, or Way of Sorrow. Each Friday a procession retraces the last walk of Christ as he bore his cross to Calvary, where the Church of the Holy Sepulchre now stands.

Modern Jerusalem

Jerusalem isn't just a sacred mystery tour of holy places. It is also a modern city full of vitality and beauty. Both Jews and Arabs have built modern additions to the city outside the old walls. The free commerce back and forth between the Arab and Jewish sides of the city adds a rich cultural mix to Jerusalem's other qualities.

The Israel Museum, opened in 1965, houses both ancient and modern treasures. Its vast complex includes museums of art and archaeology, the Shrine of the Book and a sculpture garden.

Social life and sport

For visitors of all ages, Jerusalem has its fair share of cafes, swimming pools and discotheques. It is this mix of old treasures and new pleasures that makes the city one of the most exciting in the world.

▲ The Old City as seen from across the ancient roof tops. In this quarter, which rests on the same foundations as Biblical Jerusalem, only the jungle of television antennae betrays the city's place in the twentieth century. Just outside the Old City's walls, modern Jerusalem strikes a sharp contrast.

▼ Jerusalem is an upland city, and thus much cooler and drier than Israel's Mediterranean towns. Jerusalem nights are chilly even in summer. Winter usually brings harsh rain and strong winds. Snow storms such as this are rare, and are welcomed with a holiday spirit when they come.

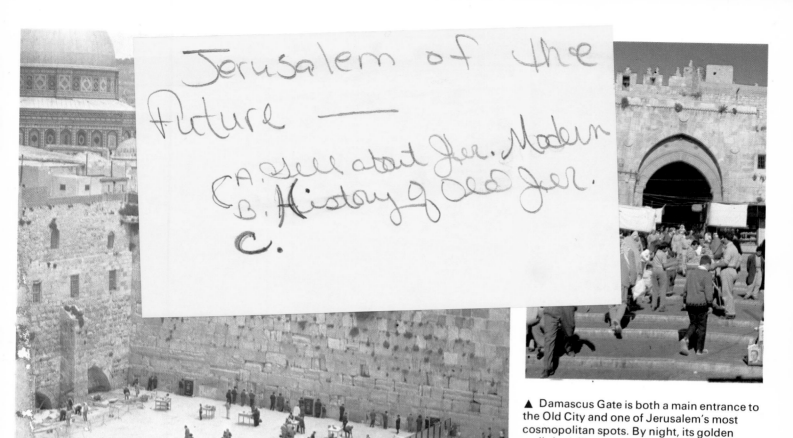

▲ Damascus Gate is both a main entrance to the Old City and one of Jerusalem's most cosmopolitan spots. By night, its golden walls look like the gateway to Camelot. By day, the crowds which rush through for worship or business are of every race and age.

This traditional view of the city shows the Jewish Western Wall, and the Muslim Dome of the Rock Mosque astride the ancient Temple Mount.

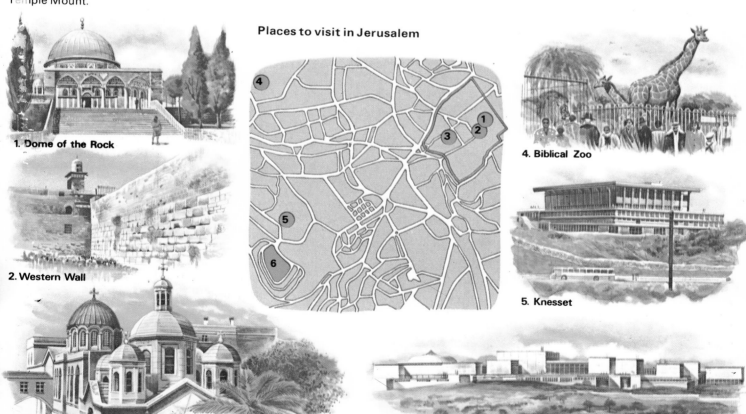

1. Dome of the Rock

2. Western Wall

3. Holy Sepulchre

Places to visit in Jerusalem

4. Biblical Zoo

5. Knesset

6. Israel Museum and Shrine of the Book

Leisure and pleasure

The centre of social life

Tel Aviv, where almost one-third of the population lives, has a continental air because of its many cafes with their tables and chairs set out on the pavements. The cafes are always full, as they are the centre of social life. Israelis are very hospitable, and they entertain each other by meeting in their favourite cafe at any time of the day or evening.

Arabs also lead a cafe life, but for them it is restricted to the men. They sit and drink Turkish coffee, smoke their pipes and chat.

A new interest in sport

Sports as we know them were not very much in evidence in Israel at first, except those brought by the British officials in the Mandatory Government, who tried to introduce cricket.

In the Hebrew University and the YMCA in Jerusalem there are a few squash courts and two or three tennis courts. Swimming is available to everyone, not only because of the sea, but because there are swimming pools in the kibbutzim and in the towns and villages.

Skiing has become more well-known since the Six Day War when Mount Hermon became part of Israel. Golf was introduced some years ago when a country club was built at Caesarea, but it is a sport

▲ Archaeology is Israel's national craze. Here, Israeli and foreign volunteers work together with scientists on Jerusalem's Temple Mount excavations.

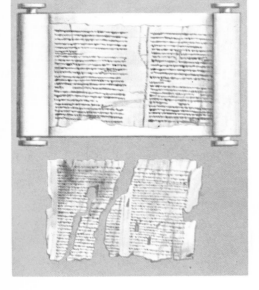

▲ Among this century's most important archaeological finds, the Dead Sea Scrolls were discovered in a cave above the north end of the Dead Sea. The Scrolls are the oldest Biblical documents ever found. They are still being interpreted. They are kept at the Israel Museum.

▼ Pony trekking in the Galilee is a new activity in Israel. It is becoming a very popular pastime with Israel's tourists, both native and foreign.

for the more well-to-do.

Football has become very popular and there are a number of teams who compete against each other before large crowds every Saturday. Some years ago an Israeli football team beat a Welsh one playing on the latter's home ground, largely because of the prowess of the Israeli goalkeeper. He was greeted on his return home as a hero.

Bible study

Shortly afterwards, an international Bible quiz of a very high standard was held in Israel. It was won triumphantly by a poor handicapped Israeli who worked as the doorkeeper in a hospital. Thousands of people came out into the streets to greet him in the early hours of the morning when the quiz finished, in the presence of the prime minister. Since then Bible study has become a national pastime and groups meet in many places regularly for the purpose.

A love of archaeology

Archaeological digs are another popular leisure occupation, and volunteers flock to help whenever a new excavation is begun. Above all, Israelis love to get together for a *kumzitz*, to drink coffee, or brandy. They chat and argue about every subject under the sun, with hot passion, but on a friendly basis, without rancour.

▲ With the Mediterranean Sea, the Red Sea, the Dead Sea and Lake Kinneret to exploit, Israel has plenty of water sports. Sailing in Eilat's harbour is very popular.

▼ Skiing is Israel's newest sport. Slopes were cleared on Mt. Hermon in the Golan Heights after the 1967 War, and the Israel Ski Club was formed.

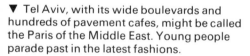

▼ Tel Aviv, with its wide boulevards and hundreds of pavement cafes, might be called the Paris of the Middle East. Young people parade past in the latest fashions.

The people of the Bible

▲ The camels and flat, black tents of the Bedouin still dot Israel's desert landscapes. Coming upon them in the midst of the desert is like stepping back into Biblical times.

The Bible as history

Though Israel is one of the world's youngest nations, it is also among the most ancient. The historical connection of the Jewish people with the land of Israel covers more than 35 centuries.

The Bible itself is the principal source of history for Israel's ancient period. It is read in Israeli schools both as a holy book and as an historical text.

The Patriarchs

According to the Bible, the Jewish nation is descended from the Patriarchs: Abraham, Isaac and Jacob, the heads of nomadic shepherd clans who believed in one God and came originally from Mesopotamia (modern Iraq).

The Bible states that God made a covenant with the Patriarchs in which He promised them and their children the land of Israel. "Israel" itself was the name given to Jacob by God. Abraham is also a Patriarch for the Arab peoples, who are said to be descended from his son Ishmael.

Exile to Egypt

Driven by famine from the land of Israel, Jacob and his sons (the Twelve Tribes of Israel) fled to Egypt. They remained there for several generations and served as Egyptian slaves.

The prophet Moses finally led the tribes of Israel out of Egypt and back to the Promised Land. Moses is the greatest leader of Jewish history. By bringing The Law from Mount Sinai, he gave cohesion and national purpose to a group of scattered tribes.

The First Temple

Under Joshua's leadership, the twelve tribes settled the land of Israel and prospered. In the eleventh century B.C. the Jews selected Saul as their first king, and he was succeeded by David. David built Jerusalem and founded a dynasty which ruled for four centuries until the Babylonian Conquest (586 B.C.) and a new exile. David's son Solomon built the First Temple, and the period takes its name from this.

The Second Temple

The exile in Babylon lasted for nearly fifty years after Nebuchadnezzar destroyed the First Temple and banished the Jews. They were allowed to return by Cyrus the Great of Persia, and rebuilt the Temple by 516 B.C. The Second Temple period, during which Jesus of Nazareth lived, lasted until 73 A.D., when the Temple was burned and Masada, the last fortress of Jewish resistance, was taken by the Romans. For the majority of Jews, two thousand years of exile followed.

▼ The land of the Bible has never known any definite borders, but this map shows the territory affected by the Biblical saga.

▼ A model of the 2nd Temple, built by 516 B.C. before the Greek invasion. It was destroyed in 70 A.D. by the Romans.

▼ King David, who ruled Israel from c. 1004-965 B.C. is said to be buried in this tomb on Jerusalem's Mount Zion.

▲ This amphitheatre at Caesarea has been rebuilt from the ruins of an ancient Roman theatre. The original was built by Herod in the first century B.C. and was used until the fourth century A.D.

▶ The excavated ruins of Masada, once Herod's royal citadel, sit as a grim reminder of the Jewish Zealots' last stand for their faith in the revolt against Rome.

▼ Elaborate figurative art distinguishes Jewish religious relics, as on this frontis-piece from the Book of Numbers.

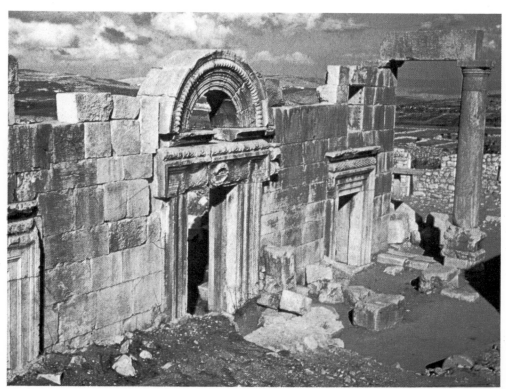

▶ Excavated ruins of the Bar-Am synagogue in Galilee, probably dating from the 4th or 5th century A.D. Israel is rich in such reminders of a vital religious past.

A succession of invaders

Greeks and Romans

Following the scattering of the Jews under Assyrian rule and the destruction of the First Temple by the Babylonians, the land of Israel was ruled for more than two thousand years by a succession of invading forces. Each left its distinctive mark on the region.

Alexander the Great's invasion in 333 B.C. was followed by 200 years of Greek rule. This coincided with the period of the Second Temple, and ended with the Roman conquest in 63 B.C. The Romans held onto power in the region for some 600 years, and were then replaced by the Arabs.

Arab rule

With the rise of Islam and the growth of Arab military might, the land of Israel was conquered by Muslim armies in 634 A.D. Islamic rule remained almost unchallenged until World War I.

Some of the Jews who had been persecuted and driven into exile under Roman rule found themselves welcome to return once the Arab armies had gained control. The Arabs and Jews coexisted peacefully and with mutual tolerance through most of the ensuing centuries.

Crusader invasion

The first great threat to Muslim rule came from the Crusaders. Inspired by adventure and an appeal from Pope Urban II to rescue the Holy Land, the Crusader Christian armies marched across Europe and during the eleventh and twelfth centuries captured most of Biblical Israel. They were seriously routed by the Arab armies of Saladin, but many fortresses remain today as a reminder of the Crusader presence.

Ottoman rule

The fall of the Crusaders in the thirteenth century led to 200 years of Mameluke rule. The Mamelukes were Caucasian slaves who had seized power in Egypt and then conquered Palestine. But in 1517, Selim I of the Turkish Ottoman Empire conquered northern Syria and Palestine. His son, Suleiman the Magnificent, destroyed all trace of Mameluke rule, and the Ottomans stayed on until 1917.

▼ The golden Dome of the Rock (Mosque of Omar) dominates Jerusalem's skyline as a perpetual monument to the Muslim presence.

▲ Arab horsemen of the Muslim armies marching into Jerusalem in 638 A.D. They defended and won the Holy Land for Islam in a 200-years war with the Crusaders.

▼ Eight times, between 1095 and the mid-15th century, Christian armies set out to regain the Holy Land from Muslim rule. The map shows the main routes of the Crusades.

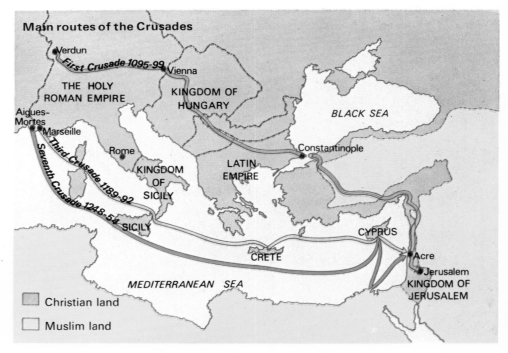

Main routes of the Crusades

Verdun
First Crusade 1095-99
Vienna
THE HOLY ROMAN EMPIRE
KINGDOM OF HUNGARY
BLACK SEA
Aigues-Mortes
Marseille
Rome
Constantinople
LATIN EMPIRE
Third Crusade 1189-92
Seventh Crusade 1248-54
KINGDOM OF SICILY
CYPRUS
CRETE
Acre
SICILY
Jerusalem
MEDITERRANEAN SEA
KINGDOM OF JERUSALEM

☐ Christian land
☐ Muslim land

▲ King Richard I of England, who led the Third Crusade, and the great Muslim warrior Saladin were the most romantic figures of the Crusader period. Richard was the better soldier, but Saladin a superior statesman.

▶ Each time the Crusader armies conquered a new section of the Holy Land, they fortified their position with a castle. This fortress in Galilee still stands as a reminder of the Christian conquests.

▼ The renowned Turkish sultan, Suleiman the Magnificent, ruled the Ottoman Empire from 1520-1566. No sovereign in Ottoman history equalled his wisdom or bravery. Under his rule, the Empire grew and was well-managed.

▶ This mosque was built by Ahmad el-Jazzar ("the Butcher"), a Turkish governor of Acre in the 18th century. During his rule, Acre was besieged by Napoleon but the town was saved by the arrival of British warships.

The Zionist awakening

▲ Theodor Herzl, an Austrian journalist and man of letters, was the founder of the World Zionist Movement. He transformed romantic dreams of a Jewish homeland into political action.

Jewish nationalism

In the nineteenth century, nationalist feeling was running high throughout Europe. Italy and Germany first became united nation states, and others were to follow. For Europe's Jews, this movement took shape in the form of Zionism—the desire to form a Jewish nation state.

Pogroms and persecution

Zionism might never have caught on among intellectual Jews, whose support it was to need, had it not been for the rise of anti-Semitism in Europe once again in the late nineteenth century.

Just as Western European Jews were beginning to enjoy the first taste of full citizenship and emancipation, the trial of the Jewish Captain Dreyfus in France shocked many people. Dreyfus, a loyal officer, was convicted of treason and sent to Devil's Island to satisfy the anti-Semitic feeling running high in France.

Theodor Herzl

It was the Dreyfus trial which produced Zionism's first great political leader. Theodor Herzl was a successful Austrian journalist. His coverage of the trial changed his life. He became convinced that Jews would never know peace and security until they had their own state.

First Zionist Congress

Until Herzl's active political struggle, the desire to return to Zion had been mostly a dream of religious faith among Jews. Now it became a real possibility. In 1897, the first Zionist Congress was held in Basle, Switzerland. A resolution was passed by delegates from around the world to recreate a Jewish state in Palestine.

Britain's Joseph Chamberlain took Zionist aims seriously enough to offer a large section of British territory, in what is now Uganda, for the Jewish homeland. But the World Zionist Organization rejected this solution on religious and historical grounds.

First and Second Aliyah

The various waves of Jewish immigration to Palestine began in 1882, and each was known as an *Aliyah*, or "ascent" to the land of Israel. The first *Aliyah* was funded largely by Baron de Rothschild, but it adopted traditional colonialist settlement policies. The second *Aliyah*, which consisted mostly of idealistic socialist Jews from Russia, fashioned the institutions and values that shaped the modern State of Israel.

The Balfour Declaration

In 1917, persuaded by the scientist Chaim Weizmann, prime minister David Lloyd George became convinced that the Zionist dream was in Britain's own best interests. In November 1917, Lord Balfour pledged the British government to use their best endeavours to establish a national home for the Jewish people in Palestine.

▼ At the 2nd Zionist Conference in Basle, Switzerland, delegates from all over the world debated measures needed to establish the Jewish homeland.

▼ Chaim Weizmann, later first president of the new State of Israel, wore Arab dress to hold talks with the Emir Faisal, King Hussein's grandfather in 1918.

▼ The Baron Edmonde de Rothschild, one of the world's richest Jews, favoured the Zionist movement and gave vast sums to help the early settlers.

▲ Once news of the new homeland spread among Europe's Jewish communities, many means of getting there were tried. These Russian immigrants walked all the way.

▼ The Russian pioneers of the second *Aliyah* came with the ideal of hard labour building a new society. Many had to clear fields like this single-handed.

Independence

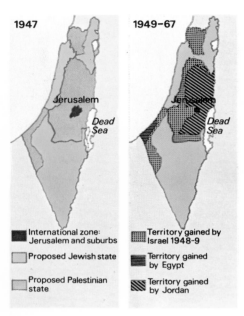

1947   1949-67

Jerusalem · Dead Sea

International zone: Jerusalem and suburbs

Proposed Jewish state

Proposed Palestinian state

Territory gained by Israel 1948-9

Territory gained by Egypt

Territory gained by Jordan

▲ Israel's borders have never remained fixed. A succession of wars and political settlements have left the map maker's task virtually impossible. The 1947 map shows the original United Nations intention to divide Palestine into a small independent Jewish state and a small Palestinian Arab state. After the Arab invasion in 1948 and the subsequent war, the boundaries stood as shown on the second map.

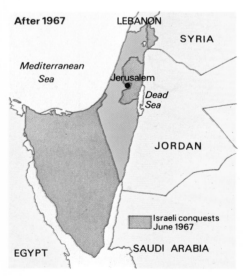

After 1967

LEBANON · SYRIA · Mediterranean Sea · Jerusalem · Dead Sea · JORDAN · Israeli conquests June 1967 · EGYPT · SAUDI ARABIA

▲ The 1967 Six Day War altered the boundaries again, and this map shows the present position, though political debate continues. The Sinai Peninsula, the Gaza Strip and the West Bank of the Jordan are currently administered by the Israeli government while politicians decide their fate. Palestinian Arabs want at least the West Bank and Gaza for their own homeland.

British Mandate

Britain had taken over rule of Palestine from the Turks after the First World War. The British ruled the area until the United Nations partition plan was announced in 1947. But during the Mandate period, the barely disguised civil war between Palestine's Arab and Jewish communities grew increasingly violent.

Riots and terrorism

In 1936-39, as Hitler began massacring European Jews by the millions, the worst anti-Jewish riots occurred in Palestine. Hundreds were killed by Arab gangs in Jerusalem and the outlying kibbutzim.

This was the period when the Israel defence forces began in rough form. The Haganah, later to become the backbone of today's army, was the mainstream force. The Palmach was an elitist, left-wing strike force trained in commando-style operations by Britain's General Orde Wingate. On the far right, the Lehi, or Stern Gang, were a band of Jewish terrorists who were led by Abraham Stern and specialized in assassination.

World War Two

During the Second World War, many Jewish soldiers joined the British army and navy to fight their common foe, the Nazis. Some Arabs also volunteered, but many of their leaders maintained friendly relations with Germany and this led to greater tension between the Jews and Arabs of Palestine for years to come.

Independence

On May 14th, 1948, Israel declared itself an independent state. Within 24 hours, while jubilant throngs were still dancing in the streets, the new nation was invaded by the combined armies of Egypt, Jordan, Syria, Lebanon and Iraq.

The Israelis fought the invasion with everything they had: a few old planes left behind by the British forces, whatever guns could be found from here and there, and ingenious devices often put together out of gunpowder and chicken wire.

Hostilities finally ceased in January, 1949, with the Arab armies defeated. But Israel had lost nearly a quarter of her population in the Independence war. At the same time, the full measure of the European holocaust was realised, and the shock of the deaths of six million Jews was felt deeply. Israel still suffers from memories of those combined losses, and they probably explain the streak of melancholy fatalism that sometimes shows itself in the Israeli character.

Building a new nation

Largely with the force of his own personality, David Ben-Gurion rallied the spirits of Israeli's new citizens and began the task of building the new nation.

▼ The Independence brought Jewish refugees to Israel from the detention camps. Such ships arrived constantly.

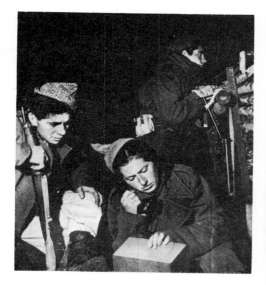

▲ Men and women of the Haganah used phones and guns in the trenches during the 1948 War of Independence.

▲ The King David Hotel was used as military headquarters by the British army. It became a casualty of Jewish terrorism when one wing was bombed.

◄ As the refugees from the concentration camps of World War II poured into the new state, most had to be accommodated in temporary tent cities.

▼ On November 29th, 1947, the U.N. voted to create a State of Israel. The crowds waiting in a Tel Aviv square celebrated when the deciding vote was cast.

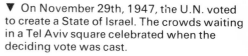

▲ David Ben-Gurion, Zionist pioneer and leader of his people for more than half a century. Without him there might never have been a State of Israel.

The arts

Painting and sculpture

In Israel's early years, forms of art were mainly imported from abroad. Today, however, there are growing numbers of Israeli-born musicians, painters, composers and playwrights whose works are known internationally.

In 1906 the first museum and art school were opened in Jerusalem. In 1965 the Israel National Museum was built with help in funds and exhibits from abroad. It includes the Billy Rose Art Garden of modern sculpture, the Samuel Bronfman Biblical and Archaeological Museum, a youth wing, and the Shrine of the Book which houses the Dead Sea Scrolls, Israel's most priceless possession.

Tel Aviv opened its first museum in 1926. It was rebuilt and enlarged in 1971, with a pavilion donated by and named after Helena Rubinstein. There is now also the Ha'aretz Museum of Mediterranean Art and other specialized pavilions. Haifa has a Museum of Modern Art, a Japanese Art Pavilion, and others.

An artists' colony, Ein Hod, has been established near Haifa, run on kibbutz principles. Artists' colonies have also grown up in the ancient cities of Safed and Jaffa, which are great tourist attractions. Many kibbutzim have their own galleries and encourage artistic talent.

Music and drama

The Israel Philharmonic Orchestra was founded in 1936 by Bronislaw Hubermann. Since then many famous players and conductors have worked with the orchestra, which is supported by 32,000 annual subscribers. There are a number of other orchestras in Israel, and a National Opera, which was founded in 1947. Newcomers to Israel have often brought different forms of dancing with them. Inbal, a Yemenite group, is an example of this.

In all, there are 29 conservatoires in Israel, with over 9,700 students. In the schools, there are 130 orchestras and 400 choirs.

The National Theatre is the Habimah, founded in 1917, which now has its own building in Tel Aviv. The Cameri became the Tel Aviv municipal theatre in 1970, and in 1961 Haifa created its own municipal theatre.

▲ A string ensemble and vocalist appear at Binyamei Ha'oma (Building of the People), Jerusalem's largest music centre and home of the Israel Symphony Orchestra.

▼ Folk dancing is popular both as an amateur pastime and as professional entertainment. This Yemenite company perform one of their traditional dances.

▲ Mordechai Ardom, one of Israel's most established artists, works in his studio. The government tries to encourage artists by developing art colonies and converting old houses into suitable studios.

▲ The Museum of Modern Art in Haifa draws visitors from all over the country. Tel Aviv is still the main centre for art galleries but more are opening in Jerusalem and Haifa. Many kibbutzim have their own galleries.

▼ Jerusalem university students look over one of the modern sculptures in the Israel Museum's collection. Such objects are found all over the museum's grounds.

▶ These stained glass windows, designed by Russian artist Marc Chagall, illustrate each of the Twelve Tribes of Israel. They are among Israel's great art treasures.

▼ When he died, American artist Billy Rose donated his entire sculpture collection to Jerusalem's Israel Museum. The Billy Rose Sculpture Garden ranks highly as a modern art treasure.

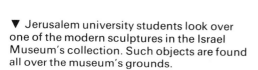

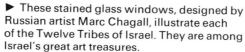

Industry and crafts

▼ These Bedouin Arab women are spinning dyed wool in the traditional manner.

▲ A Yemenite silversmith bends over his painstakingly delicate art. Such ancient crafts still flourish in Israel.

Industrial expansion

Israel's industrial production rose in 1968 by 29 per cent, in 1969 by 16 per cent and in 1970-72 by an average of 12 per cent. Industrial exports, other than diamonds, have grown tenfold since the Fifties to a value of 650 million dollars in 1973. With diamonds this figure amounts to 1,273 million dollars.

A dramatic change in Israeli industry came about after the Six Day War, when France, previously Israel's biggest supplier of arms, pronounced an embargo. Israel had to rely heavily on itself and there was a speedy development in the electric and electronic products industry. This industry now accounts for ten per cent of total industrial production.

The aircraft industry, which began as a plant to assemble imported parts, is now producing wholly Israeli-made aircraft, some of which are exported. Diamonds are the next most important industry. They are imported rough and are cut and polished before being exported. The industry is centred in Netanya but smaller plants exist elsewhere. In 1973 diamonds to the value of 623 million dollars were exported and netted 83 million dollars profits.

Textiles and garment factories were set up in the Fifties, when cotton began to be grown in many areas, and work had to be found for new immigrants. Israeli-made clothes are exhibited in many fashion shows abroad and are exported in considerable quantities.

The extraction of minerals

The only significant mineral found in Israel is copper, in the Timna mines near Eilat. Phosphates are extracted from deposits at Oron. These are mainly used for fertilizers.

Potash is extracted from the Dead Sea at a plant which was originally started by a well-known Russian engineer and then taken over by the government after Israel became a state. To process and market these minerals, a large chemical complex was established at Arad, a new town in the Negev, involving an investment of 200 million Israeli pounds.

Investment in industry and crafts

Government policy is directed to encouraging investors from abroad, and both the government and the General Federation of Labour (equivalent to the TUC in Britain) also invest largely in Industry.

Communal workshops producing beautiful jewellery and objets d'art by Yemenites and North Africans are supported. These workshops provide employment and also maintain traditional skills.

▼ An Arab artist works with olivewood to carve religious figurines. Olivewood craft articles are popular with Israel's tourists, and are a major industry among the Arab population. Bethlehem and Nazareth produce most.

◄ This desalination plant is a symbol of Israel's constant battle to reclaim the vast desert areas within her borders. Israel has pioneered desalination techniques now being adopted by other nations which need to use their sea water.

► The Technion in Haifa is Israel's institute of applied science. Research done here forms the backbone of industrial development. The work being done by these scientists in an aeronautics laboratory will very quickly become reality in an aircraft factory.

▼ The Israel Aircraft Industries at Lod is now Israel's largest single industrial enterprise, employing over 14,000 people. The plant has produced the first all-Israeli aircraft, the Arava plane and Commodore jet, as well as the much famed Gabriel strike missile.

Agriculture and the kibbutz

▲ Babies are looked after by trained nurses in the Infants' House. They spend several hours each day with their mothers.

▲ Meal time in the Children's House at Kibbutz Suba. Children live with their own age group in houses that contain both dining and classrooms.

▲ Adult kibbutzniks take lunch in the dining hall during the noon workbreak. Kibbutz members take all their meals together, and the canteen is centre of social life.

Symbol of the nation

Though only two per cent of Israel's present population actually live on kibbutzim, the kibbutz as an institution shaped the ideals and thinking of Israel as a whole. To the world at large, the kibbutz is the symbol of Israeli nationhood.

Revolutionary concept

The kibbutz, or collective farm, was the revolutionary creation of socialist Zionists from the second *Aliyah*. They saw Jewish salvation being achieved through a return to the land. A Jewish state built by Jewish labour and shared equally by all was the ideal behind the kibbutz movement. It remains so today.

Everything about the kibbutz is revolutionary. Families are very close, but they do not live together. Children live separately in children's houses, while their parents live in their own bungalows. The children spend some time with their parents at the end of each day.

On the kibbutz, everything is shared. Each member works to the best of his ability, and in return the kibbutz provides all his needs—food, clothing, medical care, holidays and pocket money. If the kibbutz becomes more profitable, everyone benefits. Some of the more established kibbutzim enjoy such comforts as tennis courts and swimming pools, while new kibbutzim are quite spartan.

Vital to the nation's agriculture

Kibbutzim are very effective farms. Nearly all of Israel's agricultural products are produced on the kibbutzim, or in the sister settlements called moshavim. The moshav is similar to a kibbutz, but each family lives separately and takes a percentage of the settlement's profits.

A hard working day

Kibbutz days often begin as early as 5 a.m. Some field work, such as picking fruit, must be done before the sun gets too hot. Kibbutzniks usually work eight hours.

A work rota determines which task each member will do for a given week, and the tasks are equally distributed among men and women.

Thinking matters

Kibbutzniks take political thought and culture very seriously. Plays and concerts are frequent, and political discussions even more so. Sometimes political disagreement has been serious enough to divide kibbutzim.

Visitors are welcome

Kibbutzniks are proud of their creation, and each year thousands of foreign volunteers are welcomed as co-workers in the fields and dining halls. For kibbutzniks it is a chance to mix with the outside world. For the volunteers it is a valuable experience in group living and new agricultural methods.

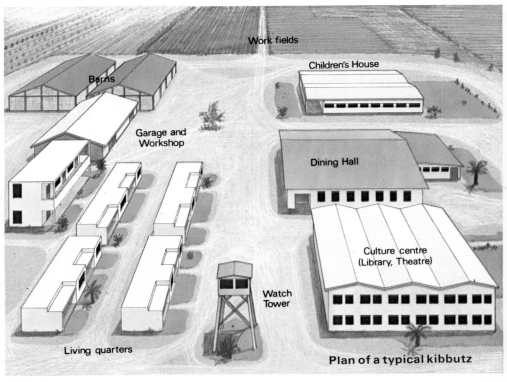

Work fields

Children's House

Barns

Garage and Workshop

Dining Hall

Culture centre (Library, Theatre)

Watch Tower

Living quarters

Plan of a typical kibbutz

▲ Democracy is taken very seriously on the kibbutz, and all decisions are made at general assemblies.

▼ Jokes abound about kibbutzniks and their cows because of the enormous pride and care they take with them.

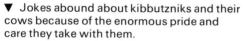

▼ Fish farming has become a major kibbutz enterprise. Members of Kibbutz Haon catch a new crop.

▲ Members of a Negev kibbutz remove melons from the protective covering used to preserve moisture in the desert.

▼ A child walks through one of his kibbutz's chicken houses. Battery raised chickens are a staple commodity.

Israel and the world

▼ El Al, which means "towards the heights", is Israel's national airline, and the international symbol of her independent statehood.

Focus of world attention

Though Israel is one of the world's smallest nations, it is constantly in the newspaper headlines. This, of course, is due to the Middle East conflict and the effect the Arab–Israeli tension has on the economies and politics of other nations.

Centre of Jewish life

For world Jewry, Israel represents the spiritual centre of its existence and holds out the promise of a kind of security that hadn't existed for 2,000 years. Should there ever be another Hitler, Jews know they would be able to find shelter in Israel.

Israel has also revitalized Jewish life. Festivals and traditions that were just managing to survive in the nations of exile are living, daily events of the new Jewish state. For the first time in thousands of years, Jews can live a full Jewish life in their own state. Jews who visit Israel only briefly find that their Jewishness is renewed.

Importance for the Third World

The agricultural, medical and technological breakthroughs Israel has had to make, in order to ensure its own survival and rapid development, are of enormous value to other developing countries.

The Israeli economy cannot support expensive foreign aid schemes, but Israeli technicians and agricultural experts devote much time both at home and abroad to teaching people from other nations who would like to learn from Israel's pioneering developments.

Israel and the Palestinians

The displacement of the Palestinian Arabs, which occurred when the state of Israel was founded, is a tragedy. Many refugees have been allowed to return, but until some political solution is found for providing a national home for the Palestinians, the Middle East will continue to be a focal point of conflict.

▼ Through their experience of draining swamps and developing new desert irrigation systems, Israelis have learned much about agriculture that can help other Third World countries.

▲ A Philippino volunteer working in the banana fields of a Galilee kibbutz. He will meet similar volunteers from other nations, and take home valuable knowledge.

► For many people, Israel is simply a lovely place to take a holiday. Israel has three sea coasts and many hotels have modern swimming pools like this one.

► Palestinian refugees return to their homes on the West Bank after the 1967 War. The "Open Bridges" policy allows Arabs from all countries to visit Israel.

▼ To people around the world, Jaffa oranges and orange juice are as much a symbol of Israel as the kibbutzim which produce them.

The Israeli army

Daring exploits

Most people have heard of the daring feats of Israel's army, such as Unit 101's rescue raid on Entebbe Airport to save hijacked air passengers, and the six day victory over the massive armies of the combined Arab world. But the bravery and fighting capacity of Zahal (Israel Defence Forces) is only one aspect of what distinguishes the Israeli army.

A citizens' army

Zahal is a citizens' army in every sense of the word, and plays a unique role as a force for education and social integration within the state.

Everyone, except the handicapped and the extremely religious, must serve army duty. At the age of 18, boys are recruited for 3 years and girls for 20 months. After that, all men must do 30 days reserve duty each year until they are 55, and unmarried women until they are 34.

There is little of the traditional military discipline in Zahal. Soldiers all wear a common uniform, but hair styles, beards and jewellery are a matter of personal taste

Army education

It is often in the army that young Israelis of different backgrounds first mix with each other. Those who need special training or education are given it, either before or after their active service.

Arab units

Arabs were never conscripted into Israel's army, but many complained of being left out. In response, Zahal now has special units for Druses and Arabs who wish to join up.

Farmer-soldiers

Nahal is a special unit inside the army for young people who want to do their active duty as farmer-soldiers in dangerous border settlements.

▲ Young women recruits from the Nahal (farmer-soldier) brigade lay barbed wire to protect their fields in Nahal Golan.

▼ These young soldiers cleaning their guns outside a barracks illustrate the lack of uniformity in army dress codes.

▲ Army duties encompass every aspect of life. This soldier is teaching an illiterate adult immigrant to read as part of the army's vast education programme. New recruits, who are themselves new immigrants, often must be taught basic Hebrew as part of their army training.

◄ An active duty unit patrols the sensitive Israeli-Syrian border in the Golan Heights. Border clashes here and along the Lebanese border are frequent. Patrol units must go out each morning to check for land mines planted by terrorists.

▲ Independence Day is always marked by a long parade in Jerusalem. Here, soldiers join in the march past that also includes school children and civilian groups.

◄ Women recruits no longer actually join in active combat, but they must undergo the same training as men. In wartime, they act as nurses and radio operators.

51

Hopes for the future

▲ A traffic policewoman helps pedestrians across a busy city street. Israel hasn't been spared the modern horrors of increased road traffic, accidents and commuter congestion.

▶ Factory production lines have become a common sight as Israel's manufacturing industries grow. Cars are not a major native product, but many car firms from abroad operate assembly plants in Israel.

▲ In a developing country, science and technology become vital assets. Israeli youth are encouraged to study science, and this holiday programme at the Weizmann Institute augments school studies.

Thirty years of development

If an Israeli returns home after a month's business or holiday, he will find that some change has taken place while he was away. For tourists who visit Israel only now and then, the country is almost unrecognizable from one stay to the next.

No country in history has ever developed so quickly or changed so much as Israel has in its thirty years of independence. From a scattered, poorly-housed population burdened with malaria-ridden swamps and unusable desert expanses, Israel has become the most highly developed nation in the Middle East. Communications media that were almost non-existent in 1948 are today a model for developing countries. The kibbutzim have produced agricultural advances.

A new people

Perhaps the greatest change taking place in Israel is in the people themselves. The immigrants still arrive by the tens of thousands, but at the same time a new, native-born population is finding its proper role in the new nation. *Sabras* are not like their parent generation from the scattered Jewish communities around the world. The Middle East is their natural home, and Arabs their natural neighbours. Most native-born Israelis know that peace with the Arab states must be part of their future.

New towns

Israel's landscape is also constantly changing. New industries spring up and as new immigrants arrive to work in them, new towns are built to accommodate them. The programme for building new towns and distributing the population out of overcrowded cities is a high government priority.

A new outlook

Israel's intellectual and cultural landscape is also changing quickly. Israelis love to learn from other people, but they are gaining self-confidence as a nation to develop their own styles in fashion, ideas and the arts. Jews who come from abroad expecting Israel to be just like their home country are often surprised to discover that Israel is unique. Most are pleased, and many never go home again.

▲ The modern Red Sea port of Eilat, nestled among the mountains of Sinai, is just one of Israel's thriving new towns. The development of new towns is a national priority.

► Since the 1967 Six Day War opened the borders between Israel and the West Bank, commerce between Israelis and Palestinians has helped understanding grow. Soldiers often chat with local Arabs.

▼ Medical facilities in Israel are among the best in the Mediterranean world. Here, young nursing candidates are taught the basics of bed-making.

▼ Israel's first television broadcast was on Independence Day, 1968. Since then, studios and programmes have become more sophisticated.

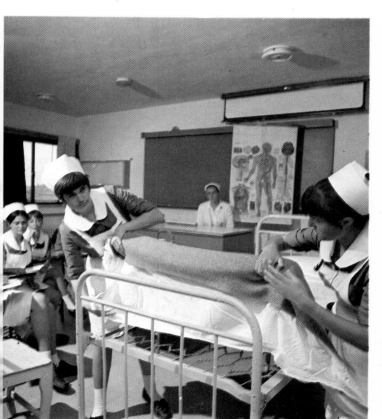

Reference
Human and physical geography

Temperature and rainfall (Jerusalem)

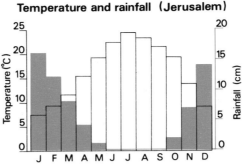

▶ There are three types of climate in Israel. Along the **coastal plain**, the winters are mild, with rainfall mostly between November and May. In the **mountains**, the winters are cold, with much rainfall and sometimes snow. In the summer the nights can be quite cool. In the **desert** and **Jordan valley**, there are mild winters, hot summers, and the nights are cold.

The climate of Israel

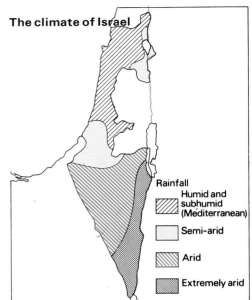

Rainfall
- Humid and subhumid (Mediterranean)
- Semi-arid
- Arid
- Extremely arid

FACTS AND FIGURES
The land and people

Position: Located on the crossroads between Asia and Africa. It has the Mediterranean on the west and Red Sea on the south.

Capital: Jerusalem.

Area: 89,359 sq. km. (34,493 sq. miles).

Population: 3,240,000 (1973).

Religions: Most Israelis are Jewish (85.1% of the population in 1973). 11.2% are Muslim, 2.4% are Christian, and Druses and other minorities account for 1.3%.

Languages: The offical language is Hebrew. Many other languages are spoken, but schoolchildren are encouraged to become fluent in Hebrew, Arabic and English.

Political system: Israel is a parliamentary democracy. The Knesset (Parliament) is elected by universal suffrage, under proportional representation.

Armed forces: Consist of a nucleus of commissioned and non-commissioned officers, a contingent called up for national service, and a Reserve. Men under 29 and women under 26 are called up for regular service. All men, and childless women, belong to the Reserves until the ages of 55 and 34 respectively.

International organizations: Israel became a member of the United Nations on May 11th, 1949. It is also a member of GATT (General Agreement on Tariffs and Trade), the International Agency for Atomic Energy, and 27 other inter-governmental organizations. In 1970, Israel signed a preferential trade agreement with the EEC, and members of the Knesset take part as observers in the work of the Council of Europe.

The natural vegetation of Israel

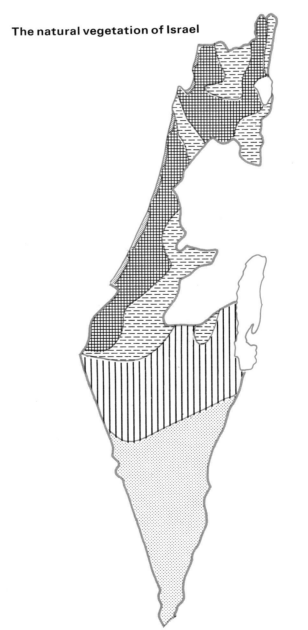

Forest Vegetation
- Mediterranean Evergreen Forest
- Mediterranean Evergreen Maquis & Meadow

Grass Vegetation
- Steppe

Desert Vegetation
- Coastal Dunes
- Desert Shrub

Population of principal towns (1973)

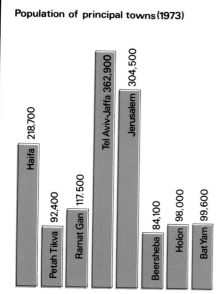

- Haifa 218,700
- Petah Tikva 92,400
- Ramat Gan 117,500
- Tel Aviv-Jaffa 362,900
- Jerusalem 304,500
- Beersheba 84,100
- Holon 98,000
- Bat Yam 99,600

Israel's population is predominantly urban. More than one-third live in the Tel Aviv-Jaffa conurbation. The government encourages people to move from the central urban region to new development towns such as Dimonah and Arad, which are designed around a comprehensive plan for housing, employment and industry.

Population density

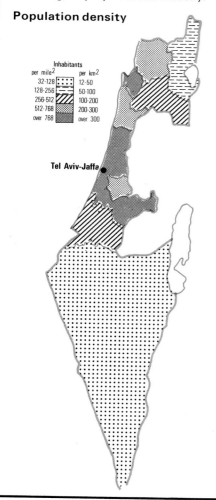

Inhabitants

per mile²	per km²
32-128	12-50
128-256	50-100
256-512	100-200
512-768	200-300
over 768	over 300

Tel Aviv-Jaffa

Government

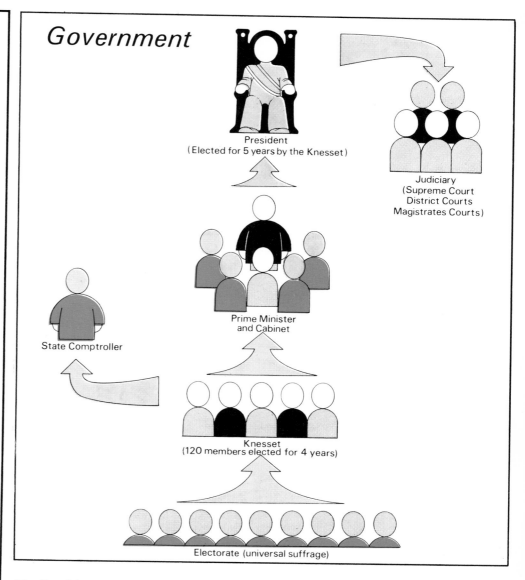

President
(Elected for 5 years by the Knesset)

Judiciary
(Supreme Court
District Courts
Magistrates Courts)

State Comptroller

Prime Minister
and Cabinet

Knesset
(120 members elected for 4 years)

Electorate (universal suffrage)

The President and Knesset

The head of State is the President, who is elected every five years by the Knesset. The President may be re-elected for one further term.

Supreme authority rests with the Knesset (Parliament), a legislative assembly with 120 members. The Knesset is elected by universal suffrage under a system of proportional representation, normally for a maximum of four years.

Under the system of proportional representation, no single party has ever had an overall majority and the country has been run by coalition governments.

The Constitution

The Transition Law of 1949 prescribed in general terms the powers of the President, the Legislature and Cabinet. In June, 1950, the Knesset resolved not to enact a formal Constitution (after attempts which failed) but to adopt basic laws as and when required, which should eventually form a Constitution.

The Law of Return

The legislation which existed when the State came into being in May, 1948, was a mosaic of laws, composed of Ottoman, British, Jewish and Roman laws. Many of these have since been amended. One of the first new laws to be passed was the Law of Return (1950) which gave to all Jews the right to live in Israel.

The Cabinet

The Cabinet, headed by the Prime Minister, is collectively responsible to the Knesset. In November, 1975, in addition to the Prime Minister, there were 20 ministers in the Cabinet.

The State Comptroller

The State Comptroller is appointed for 5 years by the President on the recommendation of the Knesset House Committee. He is responsible to the Knesset.

The State Comptroller publishes an annual report on the activities and accounts of ministries, local authorities and corporations in which the government is involved. In 1971 the State Comptroller was also given the duties of an Ombudsman, or Commissioner for Complaints by the Public.

Reference
History

MAIN EVENTS IN ISRAELI HISTORY

B.C.

c.1280 EXODUS FROM EGYPT

Slavery of the Jews in Egypt under Ramses II. Moses led them out of bondage after the ten plagues. Egyptian armies followed and were swallowed in the Red Sea, according to the Bible.

c.1250- CONQUEST OF THE LAND
1200 Joshua took over the leadership of the Hebrews after 40 years' wandering in the desert. Joshua led them to the conquest of Canaan and entry into the Promised Land, which their ancestors, Jacob and his tribes, had left to join Joseph, when there was famine in Canaan.

c.1125- THE PERIOD OF THE
1050 JUDGES
At first the Jews were ruled by judges and priests, till the time of the prophet Samuel, when they demanded a king.

c.1020- THE PERIOD OF THE
928 MONARCHY
This was the "Golden Age" of the first Jewish State. Saul was king from 1020-1004, David from 1004-965, Solomon from 965-928. Solomon built the First Temple. After Solomon's death the kingdom was split, with ten tribes in Israel, and two in the portion which became known as Judah.

928-720 ISRAEL
The first king of Israel was Jereboam I, son of Solomon. He was followed by Nadab, Baasha, Elah, Zimri, Omri, Ahab, Ahaziah, Jehoram, Jehu, Jehoahaz, Jehoash, Jereboam II, Zechariah, Shallum, Menahem, Pekahiah, Pekah, Hoshea.

722 Shalmenaeser V of Mesopotamia captured Samaria. Sargon made Samaria a province of Assyria. The mass deportation of Israelites followed and they disappeared. During the ages, various theories and claims have been put forward as to their descendants but wherever they went they were completely assimilated.

928-586 THE KINGDOM OF JUDAH
The first king was another son of Solomon, named Rehoboam, whose quarrel with Jereboam split the kingdom.
He was followed by Abijah, Asa, Jehoshophat, Jehoram, Ahaziah, Athaliah, Jehoash, Amaziah, Uzziah, Jotham, Ahaz, Hezekiah—who was considered one of the greatest of the kings and reigned c. 727-698.

701 Sennacherib sent an expedition against him but he prevailed, and he was followed by Manessah, Amon, Josiah, Jehoahaz, Jehoiakim, Jehoiachin.

597 Nebuchadnezzar conquered Jehoiachin and deported him to Babylonia and replaced him by Zedekiah.

586 Jerusalem destroyed, and mass of Jews deported to Babylonia. Some Jews escaped the net and stayed, establishing great schools of learning, parallel with the population which had gone to Babylonia where academies also flourished. Pentateuch was canonised.

538BC- THE SECOND JEWISH
70AD STATE
Cyrus, king of Persia, conquered Babylonia in 539 and issued edict permitting the return of Jews to Judah. They returned under leadership of Ezra and rebuilt the Temple in 520-515.
445 Walls around Jerusalem rebuilt under Nehemiah.

322-160 SYRO-GRECIAN ERA AND
JEWISH REBELLION
219-160 A series of conquests by Antiochus III of the Seleucids. Ptolemy IV defeated Antiochus III in the battle of Rafah and
217 recovered most of the land.

198 Battle of Banias. Land passed to Seleucids.
175 Onias (priest) deposed by Antiochus IV.
c.172 Jerusalem became a province (*Polis*) Antiochia.
169-167 Antiochus IV plundered the Temple treasuries, stormed Jerusalem, outlawed the practice of Judaism, profaned the Temple.
166-160 Judas Maccabee led a rebellion of Jews, was victorious over enemy armies.
161 He reconquered Jerusalem, reconsecrated Temple and festival of Chanukka was instituted to commemorate the victory of the few over the many. He consolidated his victory with a treaty with Rome. He fell in battle and was succeeded by Jonathan and Simeon.
142-140 Demetrius II recognised independence of Judea; treaty with Rome renewed.
134-132 War with Antiochus VII; Jerusalem besieged; treaty between John Hyrcanus and Antiochus VII.
107 John Hyrcanus' sons captured Samaria.
63-40 Civil war between Hyrcanus II and Aristobulus; Pompey captured Temple Mount and Judea lost independence.

ENTER ROME
37-34 Jerusalem captured by Herod the Great, last independent sovereign, who later became vassal of Rome.
19 Temple rebuilt.
6BC- Judea, Samaria and Idumea
41AD formed into Roman province.

A.D.

26-36 Pontius Pilate made Roman *praefectus* over Jerusalem. The prevailing, and often hostile, sects among the Jews were the Pharisees and Sadducees, but near the Dead Sea there flourished a "monastic" order of Essenes, from whom some believe Jesus Christ came, and about whom some of the Dead Sea Scrolls record.
The Jewish courts, the Sanhedrins, were the religious governors over the Jews, and before the Great Sanhedrin was brought Jesus of Nazareth, on the orders of Herod.
Jesus Christ was crucified.
66 Beginning of revolt against Rome
67 Vespasian conquered Galilee;

70	zealots took over Jerusalem. Destruction of Quamran community; siege of Jerusalem. Destruction of Temple, followed by dispersal of the Jews.
73	Fall of Masada, where Jews fought to the death rather than fall to Rome; archaeological finds confirm story.
132-135	Bar Kochba (letters of his found near Dead Sea) war.
351	Jews and Samaritans revolted against Gallus. Bet She'arim Jewish centre destroyed.

JERUSALEM AND RELIGIOUS WARS

614-617	Jewish rule established in Jerusalem under Persians.
632	Heraclius decreed enforced baptism.
638	Jerusalem conquered by Arabs.
1099	Jerusalem captured by Crusaders.
1187	Jerusalem captured by Saladin.
1244	Jerusalem captured by Khwarizans.
1516	Palestine conquered by Turks. In the following 200 years, groups of religious Jews came back to the land to settle and die, fulfilling the commandment to the Jewish people to live in the Holy Land.
1799	Napoleon's campaign.
1831	Conquest by Mohammed Ali.
1840	Turkish (Ottoman) rule established.

IN THE OTTOMAN EMPIRE

1870	First modern Jewish settlement established at Mikveh Israel.
1878	First Jewish village (now town) Petah Tikvah.
1881	First *Aliyah* (larger scale Jewish "ascent" to Palestine).
1890-1891	Large numbers of Jews come from Russia, Poland.
1904	Beginning of Second *Aliyah*, bringing new idealism of "conquest of labour". Growth of Arab nationalism.
1917	General Allenby headed British Army which captured Jerusalem; Balfour declaration issued.
1918	Zionist Commission appointed by British government to go out to Palestine.
1919-1923	Third *Aliyah*.

BRITISH RULE

1920	British Mandate accepted over Palestine. Sir Herbert (later Viscount) Samuel appointed First High Commissioner. Haganah, Jewish secret defence force, established against Arab attacks.
1922	Churchill White Paper limiting Jewish immigration to "economic absorptive capacity of the land".
1924-1932	Fourth *Aliyah*.
1929	Arab riots in Hebron and Safed.
1930	Passfield White Paper—restrictions on Jews.
1933-1939	Fifth *Aliyah* (German Jews) Macdonald White Paper, limiting Jewish immigration to total 75,000 over five years, and restricting sale of land to Jews. Lehi (Stern Gang) and Irgun Zvi Leumi, Jewish terrorists groups, formed.
1936-1938	Arab Revolt against the British.
1939-1945	Truce in struggle against British government for period of World War II.
1946	Anglo-American Committee of Inquiry appointed, recommended immigration of 100,000 Jews from Displaced Persons Camps. Rejected by British government. Flow of illegal immigrants diverted by British to Cyprus.

OVER TO UNITED NATIONS

1947	Jewish violence against British increased, as also Arab-Jewish clashes. British passed problem to U.N., who appointed UNSCOP inquiry commission. General Assembly of U.N. voted by two-thirds majority to partition Palestine into Arab and Jewish States. Plan was rejected by Palestinian Arabs.

INDEPENDENCE

1948	Proclamation of State of Israel. Arab armies immediately attacked on all sides.
1949	Armistice Agreements signed by Israel with Jordan, Egypt, Syria, Lebanon, with U.N. help. First elections to Knesset.
1956	Sinai-Suez campaign with collusion of France and Britain.
1957	Israel evacuated Sinai; U.N. Expeditionary Force sent to border.
1967	Egypt insisted on removal of U.N. Expeditionary Force. Six Day War, ending in the reunification, in Israel's hands, of Jerusalem together with Sinai, Golan Heights, and West Bank of Jordan.
1967-1973	Period of uneasy peace, war of attrition followed.
1973	Egypt attacked Israel. Syria and Jordan joined in. Ceasefire arranged and Sinai divided between Israel and Egypt. Remainder of acquired territory remained with Israel.
1974-1976	Arab terrorists struck at Israel and Jews, with Jewish retaliation. Great Powers attempted to arrange peace negotiations.

Some Hebrew words

Shalom	Peace. Used as greeting on arrival or departure
Sabra	Cactus fruit. Name for a native-born Israeli
Selicha	Pardon
Boker tov	Good morning
Erev	Evening
La'yela	Night
Chaver	Comrade, colleague
Kibbutz	Communal settlement
Moshav	Village where families are separate, but the economy is collective
Miflaga	Political party
Sa'ar	Officer or minister
Memshala	Government
Bitachon	Defence or confidence
Knesset	Assembly, parliament
Ru'ach	Air, atmosphere
Neshama	Soul, spirit
Yalda	Young girl
Yeled	Young boy
Bachura	Young woman
Bachur	Young man
Imma	Mother
Abba	Father
Dod	Uncle
Dodda	Aunt
Tinoket	Infant
Sha'ala	Question
Vakasha	Request, please
Toda	Thank you

Reference
The Economy

Agriculture in Israel

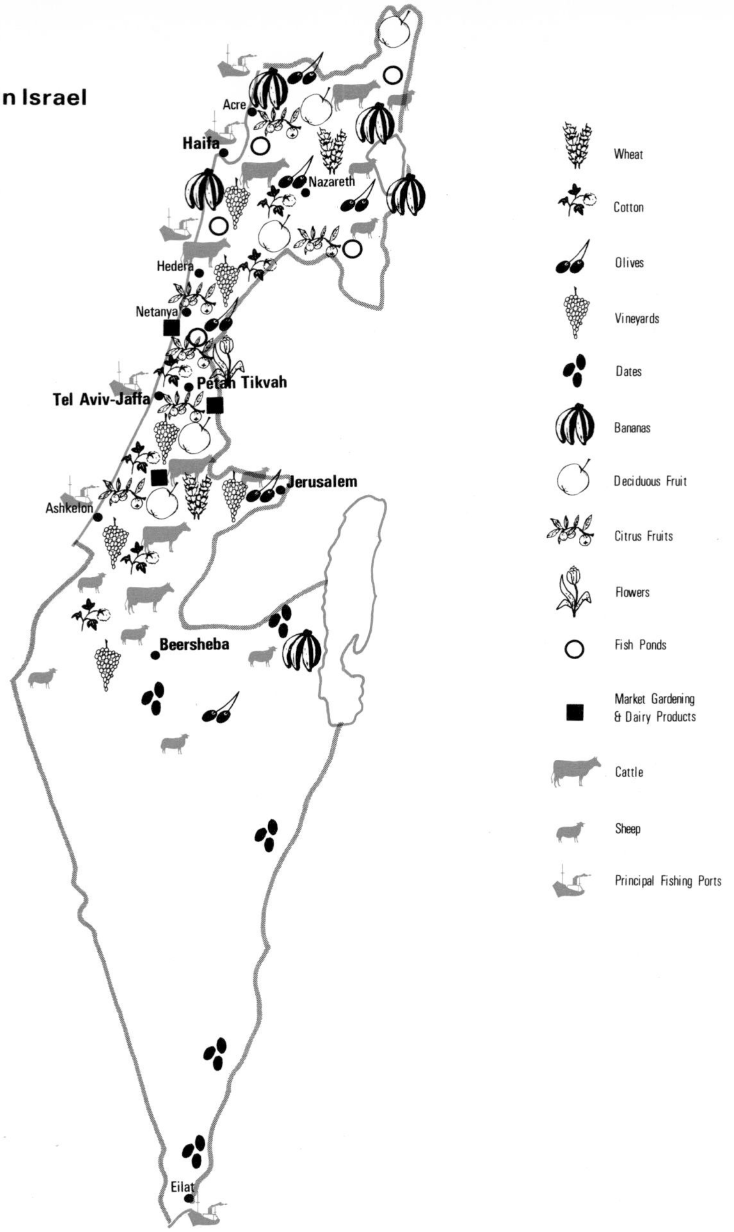

Acre
Haifa
Nazareth
Hedera
Netanya
Petah Tikvah
Tel Aviv-Jaffa
Jerusalem
Ashkelon
Beersheba
Eilat
Wheat
Cotton
Olives
Vineyards
Dates
Bananas
Deciduous Fruit
Citrus Fruits
Flowers
Fish Ponds
Market Gardening & Dairy Products
Cattle
Sheep
Principal Fishing Ports

FACTS AND FIGURES
The Economy
Gross national product: $2,300 per head.
Economic growth rate: Averages 10% per annum.
Balance of payments: The deficit on current account was expected to reach $3,000 million by the end of 1974. By the end of 1973, Israel's external debt amounted to $5,000 million. Interest payments alone on this debt reached $218 million in 1972. The debt was offset in 1972 partly by: personal restitution from West Germany ($292 million), immigrant and other private transfers ($386 million), and contributions and grants ($384 million). Only massive U.S. aid enabled Israel to pay for its increased defence outlay after the 1973 war.
Currency: One Israeli pound = 100 agorot.
Bank of Israel: Is responsible for monetary policy. The Governor is appointed by the President on Cabinet recommendation for 5 years. He acts as economic adviser to the government and has ministerial status.

Agriculture

Agriculture has been accorded special treatment, both to change the occupational structure of Jewish people and because of a need for self-sufficiency in the food supply because neighbouring states do not trade with Israel.

Fruit, vegetables, poultry, eggs, milk and dairy produce are wholly home-produced. Some of these products are also exported. Citrus fruits are one of Israel's main exports.

Cultivated areas in 1972/3 were (in thousands of hectares): Field crops: 1,690, vegetables: 260, orchards: 537, fishponds: 35, miscellaneous: 115. Shortage of water is the chief brake on further large-scale expansion of agriculture. Rain falls only in winter, and hardly at all in the southern part of Israel. Plans are being made to establish nuclear-powered installations to desalinate seawater at an economic cost.

The Ministry of Agriculture helps farmers to get credit for investment. It also provides guidance and instruction, and helps to develop marketing outlets.

Agricultural production 1948-72 (In tonnes)

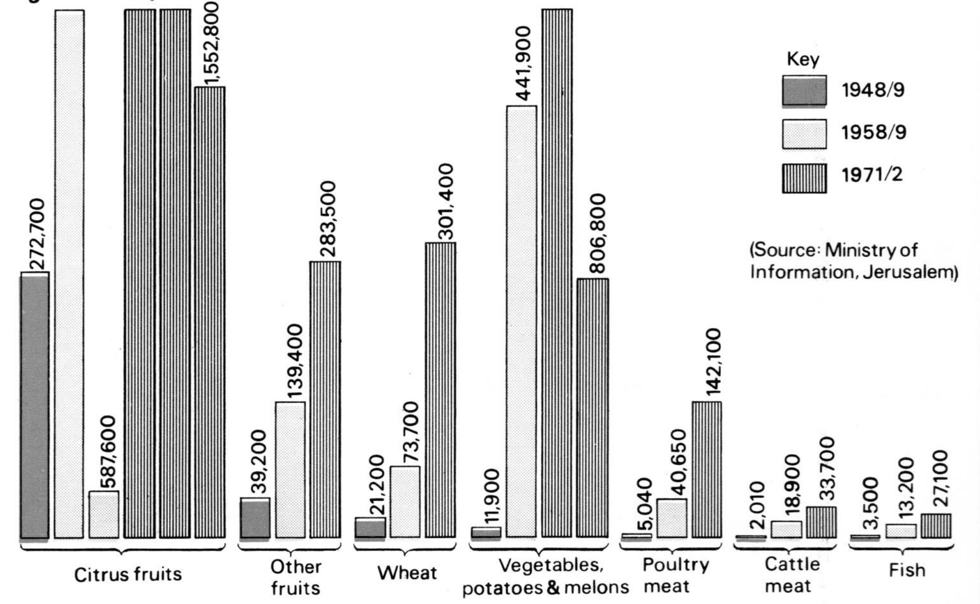

272,700
587,600
1,552,800
Citrus fruits
39,200
139,400
283,500
Other fruits
21,200
73,700
301,400
Wheat
11,900
441,900
806,800
Vegetables, potatoes & melons
5,040
40,650
142,100
Poultry meat
2,010
18,900
33,700
Cattle meat
3,500
13,200
27,100
Fish
Key
1948/9
1958/9
1971/2
(Source: Ministry of Information, Jerusalem)

How labour is employed (1972)
(as per centage of total work force)

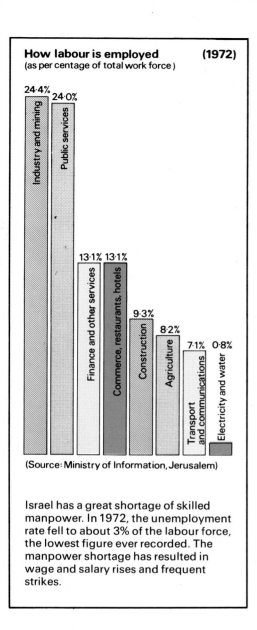

- 24·4% Industry and mining
- 24·0% Public services
- 13·1% Finance and other services
- 13·1% Commerce, restaurants, hotels
- 9·3% Construction
- 8·2% Agriculture
- 7·1% Transport and communications
- 0·8% Electricity and water

(Source: Ministry of Information, Jerusalem)

Israel has a great shortage of skilled manpower. In 1972, the unemployment rate fell to about 3% of the labour force, the lowest figure ever recorded. The manpower shortage has resulted in wage and salary rises and frequent strikes.

Industry in Israel

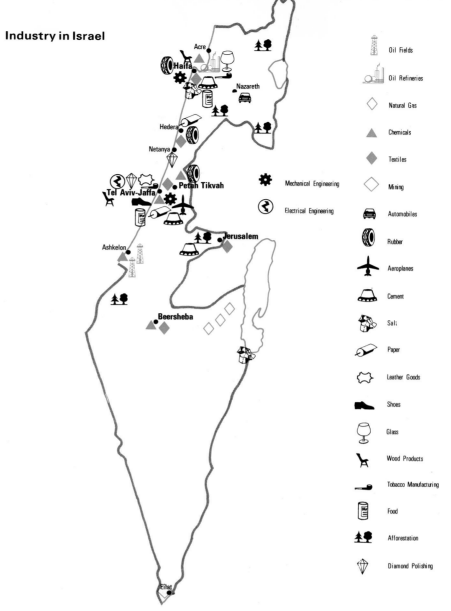

Oil Fields	
Oil Refineries	
Natural Gas	
Chemicals	
Textiles	
Mining	
Automobiles	
Rubber	
Aeroplanes	
Cement	
Salt	
Paper	
Leather Goods	
Shoes	
Glass	
Wood Products	
Tobacco Manufacturing	
Food	
Afforestation	
Diamond Polishing	

Mechanical Engineering

Electrical Engineering

Imports and exports

In 1973, Israel's gross commodity imports amounted to a total of $2,989 million. Of this, rough diamonds accounted for $488 million and investment goods amounted to $765 million. Israel's imports in 1973 came mainly from the following: the United States (20%), EEC (54%), the United Kingdom (16%).

Industrial exports, exclusive of diamonds, totalled $650 million in 1973, compared with $562 million in 1972, an increase of 16%. Diamonds accounted for $623 million in 1973, making Israel one of the world's largest producers of polished diamonds, although the cost of their import in the rough state takes a large percentage of the proceeds. The main market for diamonds is the United States.

The main customers for Israel's industrial goods are the United States and EEC countries, especially the United Kingdom and West Germany. Israel also trades with Asian countries such as Japan, Iran and Hong Kong.

Main Imports and Exports (Millions of £ sterling)

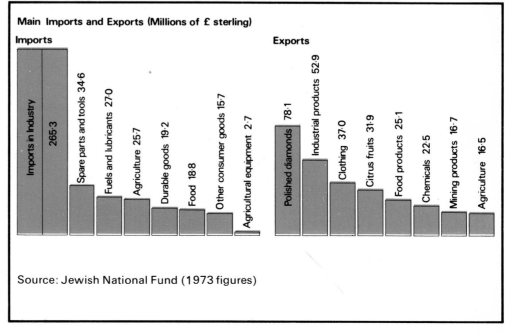

Imports
- Imports in Industry 265·3
- Spare parts and tools 34·6
- Fuels and lubricants 27·0
- Agriculture 25·7
- Durable goods 19·2
- Food 18·8
- Other consumer goods 15·7
- Agricultural equipment 2·7

Exports
- Polished diamonds 78·1
- Industrial products 52·9
- Clothing 37·0
- Citrus fruits 31·9
- Food products 25·1
- Chemicals 22·5
- Mining products 16·7
- Agriculture 16·5

Source: Jewish National Fund (1973 figures)

Gazetteer

Akko (Acre) (32 56N 35 4E) Pop. 34,400. Port city in northern Israel built as a Crusader fortress, which later became an important trade centre between East and West. Napoleon besieged the town in the 18th century but failed to conquer it.

Arad (31 16N 35 13E) Pop. 5,450. New town in the north-eastern Negev which is a flourishing centre of Negev industry and study.

Beersheba (31 15N 34 48E) Pop. 84,100. Capital city of the Negev located on southern border of Judaea. The population is a heterogeneous mixture of immigrants, and the city is a centre of mineral and textile industries. Several academic, scientific and cultural institutions, including a university.

Bethlehem (31 42N 35 12E) Pop. 14,439 (1967). City in Judaea 8 km. (5 miles) south of Jerusalem in the Administered Area and settled mainly by Muslim and Christian Arabs. In Biblical tradition the birthplace of King David and Jesus. The modern city depends largely on agriculture and tourism for its livelihood.

Dead Sea (31 30N 35 25E) Inland salt lake which forms eastern border of central Israel. About 80 km. (50 miles) long and 18 km. (11 miles) wide. Lies 392 m. (1,286 ft) below Mediterranean sea level and is the lowest point on earth. Site of caves where Dead Sea Scrolls were found, and focal point throughout Biblical history for religious sects and activities. Today a tourist spot known for its healing waters, and an important source of minerals.

Deganyah (32 43N 35 34E) "Mother of the kibbutzim". First Jewish kibbutz founded in Palestine on land south of Lake Kinneret in 1909 by pioneers of second Aliyah.

Dimonah (31 7N 35 0E) Pop. 23,700. Town in southern Israel in central Negev hills, founded in 1955. Today has important textile industry, and is site of experimental nuclear power station.

Eilat (29 30N 34 56E) Pop. 15,900. Port and resort town on Red Sea at Israel's most southern point. First established as a civilian settlement in 1949 on site of ancient harbour town used by King Solomon. Town is Israel's gateway to East Africa and Asia. Modern economy is based on tourism, copper mining, small industries and jewellery workshops.

Ein-Gedi (31 28N 35 25E) Oasis on western shore of Dead Sea and one of most important archaeological sites in Judaean Desert. Site of modern kibbutz Ein-Gedi, founded as a Nahal post in 1953.

Gaza Strip (31 30N 34 28E) Small strip of Arab territory on south-western Mediterranean coast presently administered by Israel. Population is 360,000, the bulk of which is of Palestinian and Bedouin Arabs. Area of high citrus production. Many refugee camps.

Golan Heights (33 10N 35 30E) Range of hills rising over 305 m. (1,000 ft.) on eastern border of Galilee, which remains an issue of crucial dispute between Israel and Syria. Captured by Israel in Six Day War and still under Israeli administration. The area is settled mainly by Druse farmers.

Haifa (32 50N 35 0E) Pop. 218,700. Israel's most important port, and metropolitan centre of the north. Once a largely Arab city. Modern Haifa's heterogeneous population includes Arabs, Jews and Druses. Noted principally for its port facilities, oil refineries and naval base, the city is also an important industrial centre.

Jerusalem (31 47N 35 13E) Pop. 304,500. The historical, political and spiritual capital for modern Israel, and holy city to the faiths of Judaism, Christianity and Islam. The site of wars, strife and occupation for millenia. Modern Jerusalem was divided into Eastern (Jordanian rule) and Western (Israeli rule) sectors until 1967. Today it is an uneasily united city with a mixed Arab/Jewish population.

Jezreel Valley (32 15N 35 30E) Large valley stretching across Galilee to the Mediterranean. Known as the "granary of Israel" because of its rich farmland, but called the Gateway to Hell by the Arabs because it was once dominated by malaria-ridden swamps.

Jordan River (32 15N 35 32E) Flows the length of Israel's eastern border. It originates in the Lebanon, flows through Lake Kinneret, drops down to the Dead Sea, and then passes on to the Gulf of Aqaba and the Red Sea. A source of irrigation for both Israel and Jordan.

Judaean Hills (31 45N 35 15E) Cover the area from the foothills west of Jerusalem, the Jerusalem Corridor, and extend to the Negev Desert in the east. Region of vineyards and orchards, distinguished by vast afforestation projects.

Kinneret (Lake Tiberias, Sea of Galilee) (32 43N 35 33E) The distinguishing feature of Galilee, this fresh water lake is fed by the River Jordan. It is 212 m. (696 ft.) below sea level and 166 sq. km (64 sq. miles) in area. It is the centre of the fishing industry and is the country's largest reservoir.

Masada (31 20N 35 19E) Herod's royal citadel and last outpost of the Zealot martyrs during the Jewish revolt against Rome (66-70/73 A.D.). Situated on top of an isolated rock at edge of Judaean Desert and the Dead Sea Valley, approximately 25 km. (15 miles) south of Ein-Gedi. Site of keen archaeological interest and excavations.

Mount Carmel (32 45N 35 0E) The highest slope dominating the landscape of Haifa's Mediterranean vista, steeped in religious significance. Regarded as a refuge for the profit Elijah, Carmel became the spiritual centre of the Carmelite order. The Templars established a colony there, and the Persian sect, the Bahais, have built their shrine there.

Mount Hermon (33 25N 35 50E) The triple-peaked mountain which towers over the borders of Lebanon, Syria and Israel. It was captured by Israel in the Six Day War and has since become a popular ski resort, though it remains disputed territory between Israel and Syria.

Mount Sinai (28 40N 33 40E) Though the exact location of Biblical Mount Sinai is in doubt, the high mountain of Jebel Musa in the Sinai peninsula is generally regarded as the most likely site.

Nazareth (32 42N 35 17E) Pop. 33,300. Predominantly Arab market town in western Galilee. Known in New Testament tradition as the boyhood home of Jesus, and a focal point for Christian pilgrimage throughout centuries. An important centre for Arab life in modern Israel.

Negev Desert (30 50N 34 50E) Vast region of low population comprising 11,992 sq. km. (4,630 sq. miles)—nearly 60% of Israel's total area. It is an area of high ground and hills. Rainfall is low and vegetation sparse.

Petah Tikvah (Gateway of Hope) (32 5N 34 52E) Pop. 92,400. City in Israel's coastal plain 11 km. (7 miles) east of Tel Aviv, founded in 1870s by religious pioneers. Though it began as a moshav, Petah Tikvah achieved city status in 1939 and became a marketing centre of industrial and agricultural produce.

Red Sea (20N 39E) Sea between N.E. Africa and S.W. Asia, which forms Israel's southern border and serves as the national gateway to Africa and Asia. Site of modern port of Eilat.

Rishon le Zion (31 58N 34 47E) Pop. 51,900. City of Israel's coastal plain, founded in 1882 as one of the first Zionist settlements in Palestine. Centre of the country's wine production since 1890.

Safed (32 58N 35 29E) Small town in eastern hills of Upper Galilee. Pop. 13,200. Noted historically for its role in Jewish mystical tradition, and in modern times for its artists and craftsmen.

Samaria (32 21N 35 15E) With Judaea, Samaria makes up the region known as the West Bank, a predominantly Muslim populated territory under Israeli administration since 1967. Judaea and Samaria are today the focal point of Palestinian Arab settlement and aspirations.

Sodom (31 0N 35 20E) Non-existent city still sign-posted at edge of Dead Sea salt works, where according to Biblical tradition, Sodom and Gomorrah once stood before being destroyed by God's wrath.

Tel Aviv (Hill of Spring) (32 4N 34 45E) Present population 905,100. Israel's largest city, founded 1909 on Mediterranean coastal plain, as Jewish twin city for neighbouring Arab town of Jaffa. Though Jerusalem is the state's spiritual and political capital, Tel Aviv is the central city of industry, trade, commerce, labour relations and the arts. Its sprawling metropolitan area now reaches from Jaffa in the south to Herzliya in the north, embracing an inner ring of towns including Ramat Gan, Bnei Berak, Giv'atayim, Bat Yam and Holon.

Tiberias (32 47N 35 32E) Pop. 24,200. Tourist, fishing and market town on western edge of the Kinneret (Sea of Galilee) built as a Roman town and named after the Emperor Tiberius.

Index

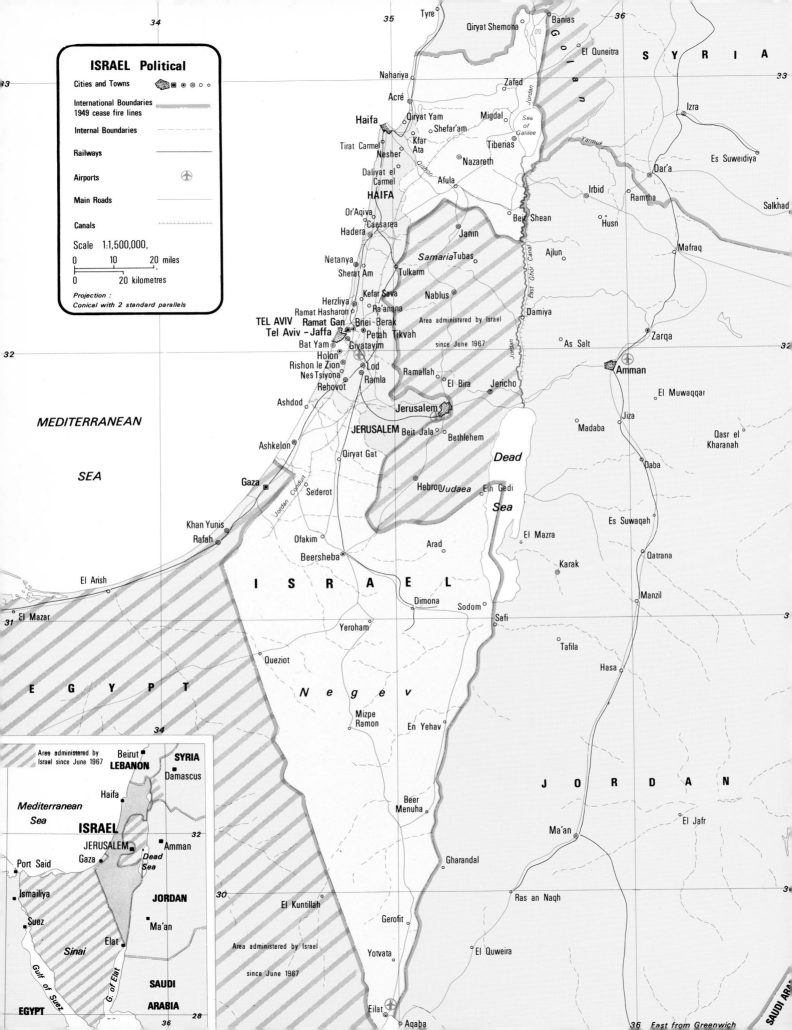

ISRAEL Political

Cities and Towns

International Boundaries
1949 cease fire lines

Internal Boundaries

Railways

Airports

Main Roads

Canals

Scale 1:1,500,000,

0   10   20 miles

0   20 kilometres

Projection :
Conical with 2 standard parallels

MEDITERRANEAN

SEA

Tyre
Qiryat Shemona
Banias
36
GOLAN
El Quneitra
SYRIA
Nahariya
Zafed
Izra
Acré
Qiryat Yam
Es Suweidiya
Haifa
Shefar'am
Migdal
Tirat Carmel
Kfar Ata
Sea of Galilee
Tiberias
Nesher
Nazareth
Yarmuk
Dar'a
Daliyat el Carmel
Afula
Qishon
Irbid
Ramtha
HAIFA
Beit Shean
Husn
Salkhad
Or'Aqiva
Janin
Ajlun
Mafraq
Caesarea
Hadera
Samaria Tubas
Netanya
Damiya
Sherat Am
Tulkarm
Nablus
As Salt
Kefar Sava
Zarqa
Herzliya
Ra'anana
Area administered by Israel
Ramat Hasharon
Amman
TEL AVIV
Ramat Gan
Bnei-Berak
since June 1967
El Muwaqqar
Tel Aviv – Jaffa
Petah Tikvah
Jordan
Bat Yam
Givatayim
Holon
Ramallah
Jiza
Rishon le Zion
Lod
El Bira
Jericho
Madaba
Qasr el Kharanah
Nes Tsiyona
Ramla
Rehovot
Jerusalem
Ashdod
JERUSALEM
Beit Jala
Bethlehem
Qaba
Ashkelon
Dead
Qiryat Gat
Es Suwaqah
Gaza
Hebron Judaea
Ein Gedi
Jordan Conduit
Sederot
Sea
El Mazra
Qatrana
Khan Yunis
Karak
Rafah
Ofakim
Arad
Manzil
Beersheba
Dimona
Sodom
El Arish
Safi
3
El Mazar
Tafila
Yeroham
Hasa
I S R A E L

Queziot

E G Y P T

N e g e v

Mizpe Ramon
En Yehav

Ma'an
El Jafr

J O R D A N

Beer Menuha

Gharandal

Area administered by Israel
El Kuntillah

Gerofit

since June 1967

El Quweira
Ras an Naqh

Yotvata

Eilat
Aqaba
E5
East from Greenwich
SAUDI ARA

(inset map)
Area administered by Israel since June 1967

Beirut
SYRIA
LEBANON
Damascus

Mediterranean Sea

Haifa

ISRAEL

JERUSALEM
Amman
Gaza
Dead Sea

Port Said

JORDAN
Ma'an

Ismailiya

Suez

Elat

Sinai

SAUDI

ARABIA

Gulf of Suez
G. of Elat

EGYPT

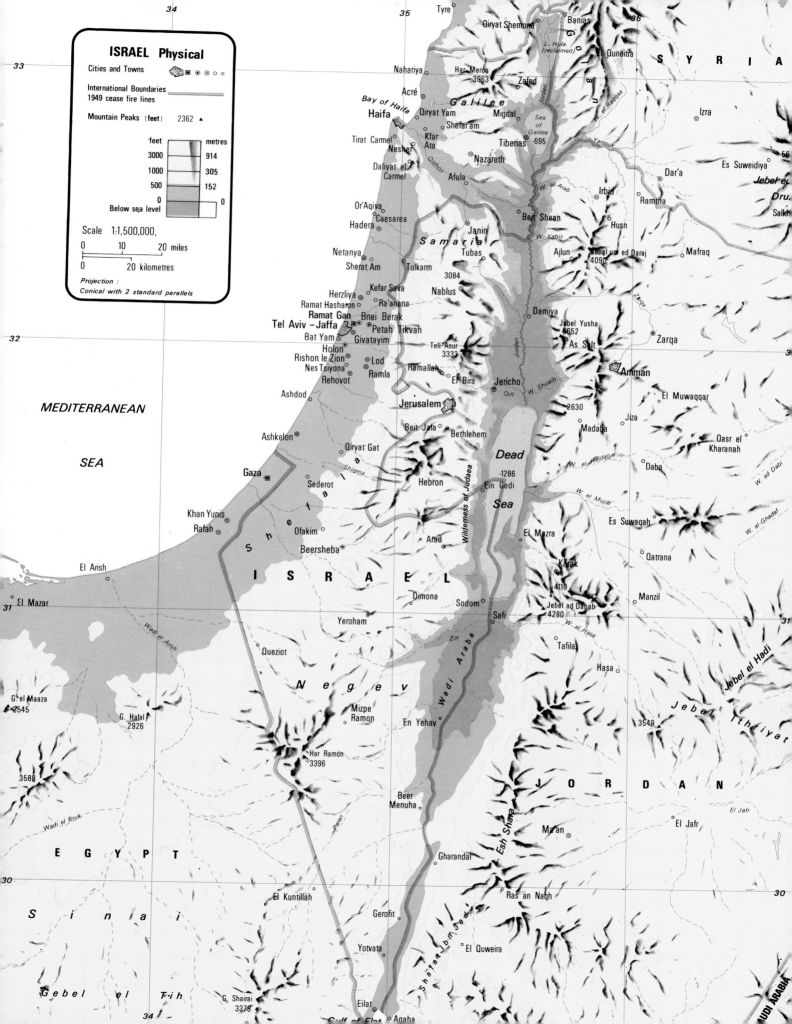

ISRAEL Physical

Cities and Towns

International Boundaries
1949 cease fire lines

Mountain Peaks (feet)   2362 ▲

feet		metres
3000		914
1000		305
500		152
0		0

Below sea level

Scale 1:1,500,000,

0   10   20 miles

0   20 kilometres

Projection :
Conical with 2 standard parallels

MEDITERRANEAN

SEA

34

35

36

Tyre

Qiryat Shemona   Banias
L. Hula   El Quneitra
(reclaimed)

SYRIA

33

Nahariya   Har Meron   Zafed
Acré   3963
Bay of Haifa   Galilee
Haifa   Qiryat Yam   Migdal   Sea of   Izra
Tirat Carmel   Shefar'am   Galilee
Nesher   Kfar   Tiberias   -695
Daliyat el   Ata   Yarmuk   Es Suweidiya
Carmel   Nazareth
Afula   W. el Arab   Dar'a   Jebel
Or'Aqiva   Dru.
Caesarea   Beit Shean   Irbid   Salkh
Hadera   Janin   Husn   Ramtha
Samaria   Tubas   Ajlun   Jebel um ed Daraj   Mafraq
Netanya   4090
Sherat Am   Tulkarm   W. Yabis
Kefar Sava   3084   Damiya   Jebel Yusha   Zarqa
Herzliya   Ra'anana   Nablus   3652   As Salt
Ramat Hasharon   Jordan
Ramat Gan   Bnei Berak   Tell 'Asur   Amman
Tel Aviv–Jaffa   Petah Tikvah   3333   El Muwaqqar
Bat Yam   Givatayim   Ramallah   Jericho   2630   Jiza
Holon   El Bira   Qilt   Madaba   Qasr el
Rishon le Zion   Lod   Jerusalem   W. Shuaib   Kharanah
Nes Tsiyona   Ramla   Daba
Rehovot   Beit Jala   Bethlehem   Dead   W. el Heidan
Ashdod   Qiryat Gat   Es Suwaqah
Ashkelon   Shigma   Hebron   Sea   W. el Mujib
Gaza   Sederot   Ein Gedi   -1286   W. ad Dabi
Khan Yunis   Ofakim   El Mazra   Qatrana
Rafah   Beersheba   Arad   Karak   Manzil
El Arish   Dimona   4110   W. al-Ghadaf
El Mazar   Sodom   Jebel ad Dabab
Yeroham   Safi   4280   Jebel el Hadi
ISRAEL   Zin   Tafila
Queziot   Wadi Araba   Hasa
Negev   Mizpe   En Yehav   3549   Jebel   Ithliyat
Ramon
G. el Maaza   Har Ramon   Esh Shara
2545   3396
G. Halal   Beer   Ma'an   El Jafr
2926   Menuha   JORDAN
3588   Paran   El Jafr
Wadi el Bruk   Gharandal   Ras an Naqb
EGYPT   El Kuntillah
Sinai   Gerofit   El Quweira
Yotvata   Eilat   Aqaba
Gebel el Tih   G. Shairai   Gulf of Elat   SAUDI ARABIA
3376

3549

30

31

32

33

34

35

36